Recent History of the Federal Republic of Germany and the United States—Recommendations for Treatment in Textbooks

Recent History of the Federal Republic of Germany and the United States— Recommendations for Treatment in Textbooks

Routledge
Taylor & Francis Group
LONDON AND NEW YORK

First published 1985 by Westview Press, Inc.

Published 2019 by Routledge
52 Vanderbilt Avenue, New York, NY 10017
2 Park Square, Milton Park, Abingdon, Oxon OX14 4RN

Routledge is an imprint of the Taylor & Francis Group, an informa business

Library of Congress Catalog Card Number: 84-52335

ISBN 13: 978-0-367-28519-7 (hbk)
ISBN 13: 978-0-367-30065-4 (pbk)

Introduction

The recommendations that follow are the product of a series of meetings of a group of German and American scholars. The deliberations at no time consisted of scholars of only one nationality. Among the scholars were American experts on German history as well as German experts on American history. What follows should, therefore, be regarded as an attempt to identify the most important events and developments in the two countries, both domestic and international. The recommendations claim neither completeness nor any deliberate exclusion of material. They are not intended to provide specific points of emphasis. Their aim is to stimulate a discussion of one or another aspect of German or U.S. postwar history or to place it in a broader context of historical perspective.

It is, of course, difficult to compress complex social processes and conditions into short sentences and suggestions. Much is missing, emphases can be shifted, and the interpretations that are contained in these recommendations or on which they are built will undoubtedly be challenged.

Structurally, the two sets of recommendations are quite different. The recommendations on German history distinguish between general descriptive passages under each heading and a supplementary series of short guides to especially important events and problem areas. This method of presentation was chosen because it was felt to be more useful, given the dearth of material on the history of the Federal Republic of Germany currently contained in American textbooks. The listings under "Problems and Issues" are meant to be stimulating and challenging and may be particularly useful for supplementary discussions. They point to areas where there is academic controversy and where a definitive interpretation was therefore not possible.

The recommendations on American history intended for German authors and scholars are more interpretative. The analyses showed that German textbooks do not fail to present U.S. postwar history as such but that there is marked unevenness, questionable emphasis, and a lack of attention to the sweeping changes that have taken place in U.S. politics and society after 1945. It was therefore less important to focus on themes than to present the entire period in an appropriate context. It should be self-evident that in these recommendations no effort was made to "resolve" controversies but rather to label them as such and to encourage their discussion.

The recommendations on German history were originally drafted in German. Presented here are translations, and like all translations, they can probably be improved; some phrases may be subject to controversy. The documents in this collection are identical to the translations published in Germany; it was considered preferable to have identical documents rather than to attempt to negotiate editorial or translation changes.

During two years of deliberations, the following scholars participated in this project; some were present at all of the sessions and others participated in a more limited way.

For the Federal Republic of Germany:

Prof. Dr. Erich Angermann
Dr. Arnold Ebel
Dr. Gerhard Fisher
Dr. Wolfgang Jacobmeyer
Prof. Dr. Hans-Adolf Jacobsen
Prof. Dr. Karl-Ernst Jeismann
Prof. Dr. Jürgen Kocka
Dr. Ulrich Littmann
Prof. Dr. Günter Moltmann
Dr. Robert Multhoff
Herr Jürgen Neubauer
Prof. Dr. Joachim Rohlfes
Dr. Hanna Schissler
Prof. Dr. Hans Süssmuth

For the United States of America:

Prof. Donald S. Detwiler
Mrs. Ilse E. Detwiler
Prof. Wolfram F. Hanrieder
Prof. Gerald R. Kleinfeld
Prof. James T. Patterson
Prof. John Anthony Scott
Mr. Richard Straus

The deliberations were conducted as a collaborative, government-sponsored study under the co-chairmanship of the German and American project directors. After the drafting of joint recommendations at a series of four conferences, the Eckert Institute issued the report. It was disavowed by three of the participants in the American project group: Prof. John Anthony Scott of the Rutgers University Law School at Newark, the senior American historian engaged in the project; Ilse E. Detwiler, M.A., researcher in history at Southern Illinois University at Carbondale; and the American co-chairman of the joint study, Prof. Donald S. Detwiler.

Contents

A. Empfehlungen zur Behandlung der Geschichte der Bundesrepublik Deutschland

Vorbemerkung zur Entstehung der Bundesrepublik Deutschland

Die Entstehung der Bundesrepublik Deutschland sollte im Zusammenhang mit der Geschichte der Weimarer Republik*, der nationalsozialistischen Herrschaft* und den Folgen des Zweiten Weltkrieges gesehen und beurteilt werden.

Wesentliche Grundzüge der politischen, wirtschaftlichen und institutionellen Struktur der Bundesrepublik Deutschland entstanden nach dem Zusammenbruch 1945 innerhalb der drei westlichen Besatzungszonen (einschließlich Berlins). Ihre rechtliche Grundlage für die Bundesrepublik Deutschland ist 1949 im Grundgesetz verankert worden.

Die Teilung und Verkleinerung Deutschlands sind in erster Linie auf die nationalsozialistische Kriegspolitik und die darauf folgenden Entscheidungen der Sieger zurückzuführen, sowie auf die tiefgreifenden politischen und wirtschaftsstrukturellen Divergenzen zwischen den drei westlichen Besatzungsmächten und der UdSSR nach 1945. Daraus resultierte eine zunehmend stärkere Trennung der SBZ von den westlichen Besatzungszonen und schließlich die Herausbildung zweier unterschiedlicher politischer, gesellschaftlicher und wirtschaftlicher Systeme in Deutschland im Jahre 1949.

Besondere Bedeutung haben in diesem Zusammenhang folgende Problemkreise (künftig „Themen und Probleme" genannt), darunter solche, die in der Wissenschaft kontrovers interpretiert werden:

- Der Zustand 1945:
  Materielle Zerstörungen (Wohnungen, Infrastruktur), Flüchtlingsbewegungen, politische und moralische Desorientierung und Not, Aufhebung der Souveränität, Auflösung der Verwaltung, Aufteilung des westlichen und mittleren Reichsgebietes in militärische Besatzungszonen und Unterstellung der Gebiete östlich von Oder und Neiße unter polnische und sowjetische Verwaltung; die Absicht der Siegermächte, Deutschland als eine wirtschaftliche und politische Einheit zu betrachten
- die Besatzungspolitik der drei Westmächte (Demilitarisierung, Kriegsverbrecherprozesse – vgl. S. 18, 24, 44 –, Entnazifizierung und Re-Edukation, Demontage, Dekartellisierung)
- Zulassung von Parteien und Gewerkschaften
- Wiederaufbau der Verwaltung und des Kommunikationssystems
- Auflösung Preußens und Neugründung von deutschen Ländern
- Währungsreform
- European Recovery Program, ERP (sog. Marshall-Plan)
- Entscheidung für „soziale Marktwirtschaft" in den drei westlichen Besatzungszonen
- Entstehung des Grundgesetzes (Initiativen und Einflußnahme der Alliierten, Parlamentarischer Rat)
- Zerfall der gemeinsamen interalliierten Verwaltung Deutschlands

---

* Zur Geschichte der nationalsozialistischen Herrschaft und der Weimarer Republik ist beabsichtigt, Empfehlungen zu einem späteren Zeitpunkt vorzulegen.

A. Recommendations Concerning the Treatment of the Federal Republic of Germany

Introductory Note on the Origins of the Federal Republic of Germany

The origins of the Federal Republic of Germany should be examined and evaluated in light of the history of the Weimar Republic*, the National Socialist regime*, and the consequences of World War II.

After the collapse in 1945, essential characteristics of the political, economic, and institutional structure of the Federal Republic of Germany emerged within the three Western zones of occupation (and the Western sectors of Berlin). In 1949 they were constitutionally anchored in the Federal Republic of Germany through inclusion in the Basic Law.

The division of Germany and its territorial losses are attributable primarily to National Socialist war policies and the consequent decisions of the victorious powers, as well as to the profound political and economic divergence, after 1945, between the three Western occupying powers on the one hand and the Soviet Union on the other. This led to a steadily increasing separation of the Soviet occupation zone from the Western zones of occupation and finally, in 1949, to the establishment of two different political, social, and economic systems in Germany.

Of particular significance in this context are the following problem areas (referred to hereafter as Problems and Issues), some of which are the subject of scholarly controversy:

- Conditions in 1945:
  Physical destruction (housing, infrastructure); movement of refugees; political and moral disorientation and misery; abrogation of sovereignty; dissolution of administrative authority; division of western and central portions of the Reich territory into military zones of occupation, and the relegation of the territories east of the Oder and Neisse to Polish and Soviet administration; the intention of the victorious powers to view the economic and political unity of Germany
- The occupation policies of the three Western powers (demilitarization, war crimes trials – see pp. 19, 25, 45, denazification and reeducation, dismantling and decartelization of industry)
- Permission for the establishment of political parties and labor unions
- Reconstruction of the civil administration and the communications network
- Dissolution of Prussia and the creation of new German states (Länder)
- Currency reform
- European Recovery Program (the Marshall Plan)
- Decision for a Social Market Economy in the three Western occupation zones
- Origins of the Basic Law (initiatives and influence of the Western Allies; the Parliamentary Council)
- Collapse of the joint inter-Allied administration of Germany

* It is intended to develop recommendations on the history of the National Socialist regime and the Weimar Republic at a later date.

I. Geschichte der Bundesrepublik Deutschland

Um die inneren Entwicklungen und Verhältnisse der Bundesrepublik Deutschland verständlich zu machen, ist es sinnvoll, nachfolgende Zusammenhänge zu behandeln:

a) Politik

Phasen der innenpolitischen Entwicklung als Abschnitte innerer Wandlungen politischer Orientierungen: Regierung Adenauer (1949–1963; CDU/CSU mit Koalitionspartnern); die Nachfolger Adenauers aus der CDU (bis 1966); große Koalition CDU/SPD (1966–1969); die sozialliberale Koalition unter Willy Brandt (bis 1974) und Helmut Schmidt (beide SPD).

Die Verfassung der Bundesrepublik Deutschland knüpft an föderalistische und liberale Traditionen der deutschen Geschichte an. Die Verankerung der Grundrechte in der Verfassung als Normen, die Gesetzgebung und Rechtsprechung binden, stärkt die Rechtsstaatlichkeit (besondere Rolle des Bundesverfassungsgerichtes). Mit der Einführung des parlamentarischen Regierungssystems nimmt die Bundesrepublik Deutschland z. T. die Tradition der Weimarer Republik auf und schließt sich demokratischen Vorbildern an. Bis 1955 war die Bundesrepublik Deutschland noch nicht souverän, sondern in ihrem innen- und außenpolitischen Handlungsspielraum durch Vorbehaltsrechte der westlichen Alliierten eingeschränkt. Danach blieb die Zuständigkeit der Westmächte für Berlin und die Deutschland als Ganzes betreffenden Fragen erhalten.

Der zentrale Faktor der politischen Willensbildung sind die Parteien („Parteienprivileg"); seit den späten sechziger Jahren wird ihr de-facto-Monopol durch gesellschaftliche Protestbewegungen herausgefordert. Außerdem nehmen Verbände, Kirchen und Medien Einfluß auf die politische Willensbildung.

Im Vergleich zur Weimarer Republik hat sich das politische System der Bundesrepublik Deutschland im ganzen gesehen als stabil und anpassungsfähig erwiesen. Das demokratische Bewußtsein hat sich zunehmend gefestigt. Es gab und gibt in der Bundesrepublik extremistische Organisationen. Sie blieben ohne größere politisch relevante Anhängerschaft; ihre Aktivitäten veranlaßten allerdings Gesetzgebung und Verwaltung zu Gegenmaßnahmen.

Themen und Probleme:

- Das Wiedervereinigungsgebot (Präambel des Grundgesetzes)** und der Sonderstatus von Berlin
- Spannungsverhältnis von Verfassungsnorm (Gewaltenteilung) und Verfassungspraxis (Problem der Verklammerung von Legislative und Exekutive)
- „Kanzlerdemokratie": Richtlinienkompetenz des Bundeskanzlers und konstruktives Mißtrauensvotum des Bundestages
- Bund-Länder-Föderalismus
- Kontinuitätsfrage (Restauration oder Neuanfang)
- Bürgerinitiativen und Protestbewegungen
- Notstandsgesetzgebung 1968, Antiterrorgesetzgebung, Abwehr von Extremisten im öffentlichen Dienst (sog. Radikalenerlaß)

b) Wirtschaft und Gesellschaft

Nach dem Kriege hat die westdeutsche Wirtschaft sich schnell erholt und einen steilen Aufschwung genommen. Dafür gibt es eine Reihe von Gründen: Die Währungsreform, die

** Vgl. Nachwort des Herausgebers zur dritten Auflage.

I. History of the Federal Republic of Germany

For an understanding of internal developments and conditions in the Federal Republic of Germany, it is useful to consider the following:

a) Politics

The phases of internal political development as stages of internal transformation in political orientation: the Adenauer government (1949–1963; CDU/CSU with coalition partners); Konrad Adenauer's successors from the CDU (to 1966); the grand coalition CDU/SPD (1966–1969); the coalition of Social Democrats and Liberals under Willy Brandt (to 1974) and Helmut Schmidt (both SPD).

The constitution of the Federal Republic of Germany draws on the federal and liberal traditions of German history. The incorporation of basic rights as constitutional norms, binding on the legislative and the judiciary, strengthens the rule of law (special role of the Federal Constitutional Court). With the introduction of the parliamentary system of government, the Federal Republic of Germany follows, in part, the tradition of the Weimar Republic, but incorporates features of other democratic models as well. Prior to 1955, the sovereignty of the Federal Republic was limited in areas of domestic and foreign policy by rights reserved to the Western Allies. Thereafter, the prerogatives of the Western powers were retained for Berlin and for matters pertaining to Germany as a whole.

The primary agents in the political articulation of the will of the people are the political parties (the "privilege of the parties", whose constitutional role is defined in the Basic Law). Since the late 1960s, their de facto monopoly has been challenged by social protest movements. The political process is also influenced by various organized groups, the churches, and the media.

In comparison to the Weimar Republic, the Federal Republic of Germany has proved, on the whole, to have a stable and adaptable political system. The level of democratic consciousness has steadily risen and matured. There have been and continue to be extremist organizations in the Federal Republic. They have not attracted a substantial political following, but their activities have led to legislative and administrative counter-measures.

Problems and Issues:

- The commitment to reunification (Preamble of the Basic Law) and the special status of Berlin
- Tensions between constitutional theory (the division of powers) and constitutional reality (problems of the linkage between the legislative and the executive)
- "Chancellor Democracy": the prerogative of the chancellor to determine policy guidelines, and the "constructive" no-confidence vote by the federal parliament (Bundestag)
- Problems in the federal relationship between the central government and the states (Länder)
- The question of historical continuity (restoration or a new beginning)
- Citizen initiatives and protest movements
- Emergency legislation of 1968; anti-terrorist laws; exclusion of extremists from public service (the so-called "radicals decree")

b) Economy and Society

After the war, the West German economy recovered quickly and took a steep upturn. There were a number of reasons for this: the currency reform; initial assistance through

Starthilfe durch das amerikanische ERP („Marshall-Plan), Entscheidung für die „soziale Marktwirtschaft" – gefördert u. a. durch ein von den USA gestaltetes globales liberales Wirtschafts- und Währungssystem –, optimale Investitionschancen infolge der Aufbausituation, hoher Ausbildungsstand und Leistungsbereitschaft der Bevölkerung, das anfänglich äußerst niedrige Lohnniveau.

Die wirtschaftliche Entwicklung wurde von den Vertriebenen sowie den Flüchtlingen aus der DDR (ca. 1/4 der Bevölkerung Ende der fünfziger Jahre) mitgetragen und war eine wichtige Voraussetzung für deren Integration in die westdeutsche Wirtschaft und Gesellschaft. Diese Bevölkerungsbewegungen führten zu einer starken landsmannschaftlichen, konfessionellen und sozialen Mischung.

Heute zählt die Bundesrepublik zu den führenden Industrienationen der Welt. Ein in den übrigen westlichen Industrieländern weithin für vorbildlich gehaltenes System sozialer Sicherung hat diese wirtschaftliche Entwicklung begleitet und ist durch sie möglich geworden. Der allgemeine Wohlstand ist ein Faktor, der die Zustimmung der westdeutschen Bevölkerung zum demokratischen System und dessen Stabilität gefördert hat.

Die Tarifautonomie von Unternehmern und Gewerkschaften hat sich als Instrument der Regelung von Arbeitskämpfen bewährt und leistet einen bedeutenden Beitrag zur Erhaltung des sozialen Friedens. Die größtenteils in einer Einheitsgewerkschaft zusammengeschlossenen Einzelgewerkschaften haben durch gesamtwirtschaftliche Verantwortung und hohe Kooperationsbereitschaft einen wichtigen Anteil am Aufschwung der westdeutschen Wirtschaft gehabt.

Der wachsende Bedarf an Arbeitskräften führte zu einem starken Zuzug ausländischer Arbeitnehmer („Gastarbeiter"; wichtigste Herkunftsländer: Türkei, Jugoslawien, Griechenland, Italien, Spanien, Portugal). Die Integration dieser Gruppen in die westdeutsche Gesellschaft ist bisher – wie auch in anderen Staaten – ungelöst und problematisch.

Themen und Probleme:

- Währungsreform (1948), investitionsfördernde Abschreibungsgesetze, bewußte Stärkung des Produktivkapitals
- Bewegungen auf dem Arbeits- und Geldmarkt (im internationalen Vergleich niedrige Inflationsraten)
- „Lastenausgleich" und andere Maßnahmen zur wirtschaftlichen Eingliederung der Vertriebenen; politische Konsequenzen dieser Integration: letztlich Scheitern einer eigenen Vertriebenenpartei, Verbindung der Proklamation von Gewaltverzicht und „Recht auf Heimat" (Charta der Heimatvertriebenen 1950)
- Beispiele für das System der sozialen Sicherung: gesetzliche Kranken- und Unfallversicherung, dynamische Altersrente, Arbeitslosenversicherung
- Exportabhängigkeit und weltwirtschaftliche Verflechtung der deutschen Industrie
- Konzentration und politischer Einfluß von Wirtschaftsunternehmen
- die Finanzierung der Sozialleistungen als Problem („Grenzen des Sozialstaates"?)
- die Mitbestimmung der Arbeitnehmer und der Gewerkschaften in den Betrieben, das Betriebsverfassungsgesetz als Schutz des Arbeitnehmers
- Einebnung krasser sozialer Statusunterschiede als Konsequenz der Mobilität und Nivellierungstendenzen durch den Zweiten Weltkrieg und seine Folgen
- Gefährdung des sozialen Friedens in Ballungsgebieten, Wohnungspolitik, Jugendarbeitslosigkeit, Spannungsverhältnis von Ökologie und Ökonomie
- gesellschaftlicher und politischer Pluralismus

America's European Recovery Program (the ERP or Marshall Plan); the decision for a free enterprise system with social responsibility ("Soziale Marktwirtschaft"), which owed its initial success in part to the global market created through the liberal economic and monetary system established under U.S. leadership; optimal investment opportunities created by the need for industrial reconstruction; generally high levels of education and productivity; and, initially, an extremely low wage level.

Refugees from the German Democratic Republic and Germans expelled from territories further east, who by the end of the 1950s constituted about a quarter of the population of the Federal Republic, made an important contribution to the economic growth which, in turn, was an important prerequisite for their integration into the West Germany economy and society. These movements of population led to a mixing of regional, religious, and social groups.

Today, the Federal Republic is one of the world's leading industrial nations. The development of a system of social security widely considered exemplary by other Western industrialized countries accompanied the economic development and was made possible by it. General prosperity is one of the factors that have contributed to the West German population's support of the democratic system and to its stability.

Collective bargaining between management and unions has proven itself as an instrument for resolving labor conflicts and makes a significant contribution to the maintenance of social tranquility. The individual unions, most of which are united in a general confederation, have played an important part in the surge of the West German economy by virtue of their sense of responsibility for the economy as a whole and by their highly cooperative attitude.

The growing need for labor led to a large influx of foreigners ("guest workers"), especially from Turkey, Yugoslavia, Greece, Italy, Spain, and Portugal. As in other countries, the social integration of these groups has so far been an unresolved problem in West Germany.

Problems and Issues:

- Currency Reform of 1948; encouragement of investment by legislation providing for tax write-offs on accelerated depreciation schedules; deliberate increase of capital investment
- Movements in the labor and currency market (an inflation rate that is low by international comparison)
- The "equalization of burdens" (federal law of 1952) and other measures for the economic integration of the expellees; political consequences of this integration: the ultimate collapse of the expellees' own political party, and linkage of the repudiation of the use of force with the proclamation of the "Right to One's Homeland" in the 1950 Charter of the Expellees
- Examples of the social security system: legally mandated health and accident insurance; old-age pensions pegged to the cost-of-living index; unemployment insurance
- Dependence on the export market and the integration of German industry into the world economy
- Concentration and political influence of commercial and industrial enterprises
- The challenge of financing social programs ("limits of the welfare state"?)
- Co-determination by employees and unions in industry; the law on the structure of industrial and commercial enterprises as a measure to protect the workers
- Levelling of major differences in social status as a consequence of population mobility and the general levelling tendencies arising from World War II and the aftermath
- Endangering of social tranquility in concentrated metropolitan areas; housing policies; youth unemployment; the tension between ecology and economy
- Pluralism in society and politics

c) Kultur und Gesellschaft

Wissenschaft und Kunst sind durch den Nationalsozialismus von der Entwicklung in der Welt abgeschnitten und an der Entfaltung gehindert worden, insbesondere durch Emigration, Berufsverbote, Verhaftung und Tod von Künstlern und Wissenschaftlern – besonders deutscher Juden. Die Entwicklung der Kunst nach 1945 ist zunächst charakterisiert durch Rezeption europäischer und amerikanischer Werke, die Aufnahme der Emigrationsliteratur und die Auseinandersetzung mit Krieg, Nationalsozialismus und Flüchtlingsschicksal. Die Entwicklung der Bundesrepublik wurde von einer intensiven literarischen Auseinandersetzung mit sozialen und politischen Themen begleitet und beeinflußt. Ein bestimmender kultureller Mittelpunkt, wie er in Berlin in den zwanziger Jahren bestand, hat sich nicht herausbilden können.

Die Wissenschaft wird vornehmlich durch den Staat an Universitäten und Forschungsinstituten gefördert. Kriegsbedingte Verluste an Menschen und Einrichtungen ließen in einer Reihe von Disziplinen die Forschung nur langsam den Anschluß an internationale Standards wiedergewinnen.

Das Erziehungswesen der Bundesrepublik wurde nach dem Kriege unter Einflußnahme der Alliierten wieder aufgebaut und seit Mitte der sechziger Jahre erheblich reformiert. Ziele waren vor allem der erweiterte Zugang zu den Institutionen höherer Bildung und die Modernisierung der Curricula im Hinblick auf Chancengleichheit und gesellschaftliche Bedürfnisse. Zur gleichen Zeit erfolgte ein starker Ausbau der alten und die Gründung zahlreicher neuer Hochschulen und Universitäten.

Nach dem Kriege galt das Interesse vornehmlich dem wirtschaftlichen Aufbau und der Herstellung stabiler politischer Institutionen. Eine sich mit dem Erfolg einstellende Selbstzufriedenheit wurde seit Mitte der sechziger Jahre zunehmend durch Kritik an sozialen und politischen Verhältnissen und vorherrschenden Wertvorstellungen in Frage gestellt. Diese Kritik führte zu einer gewissen Erschütterung von Amtsautorität, brachte unter dem Stichwort der Emanzipation in vielen Bereichen mehr Partizipation, führte aber auch zu Spannungen zwischen Generationen, Geschlechtern, am Ausbildungsplatz, in Schulen und Universitäten. Nicht beabsichtigte Folgen stellten sich vor allem durch Ausdehnung bürokratischer Zuständigkeiten ein. Im Zusammenhang mit der politischen Wende (Beginn der sozialliberalen Koalition 1969, wirtschaftlicher Rezessionen und außenpolitischer Spannungen) machte es der Mentalitätswandel in der Bundesrepublik schwieriger, den politischen und sozialen Grundkonsens in der Gesellschaft aufrechtzuerhalten.

Themen und Probleme:

- Stellung und Funktion der Kirchen im öffentlichen Leben: Dominanz der beiden großen Kirchen (Katholiken, Protestanten) und ihr Einfluß im öffentlichen politischen Bereich; ihre soziale und karitative Bedeutung, ihr Einfluß im Erziehungswesen; Ausgleich der Spannungen zwischen den Konfessionen durch die Ökumenische Bewegung
- Förderung der kulturellen und wissenschaftlichen Verbindung mit dem Ausland durch die westlichen Alliierten, durch Amerikahäuser, „Brücke“, deutsch-französisches Jugendwerk, Austauschprogramme für Schüler, Studenten und Wissenschaftler
- im Grundgesetz verankerte Freiheit von Kunst und Wissenschaft; beträchtliche öffentliche Subventionierung; Kulturhoheit der Länder
- Anstieg der Schülerzahlen der höheren Schule und der zum Studium berechtigenden Abschlüsse von ca. 5 % (1950) auf ca. 20–25 % (1980). Das Problem der Abstimmung des Ausbildungssystems mit dem Beschäftigungssystem

c) Culture and Society

Under National Socialism, the arts and sciences became isolated from international developments and were prevented from flourishing in Germany, particularly because many artists, writers, scholars, and scientists, above all German Jews, were forbidden to practice their profession, compelled to emigrate, arrested, or put to death. Developments after 1945 were initially characterized by a receptiveness of work from Europe and America, by the acceptance of the literature of those who had emigrated and by a discussion of war, National Socialism, and the fate of the refugees. The growth of the Federal Republic was accompanied and influenced by an intense literary discussion of social and political themes. A single influential cultural center, such as Berlin had been in the 1920s, has not emerged.

Advanced scholarship and research is subsidized primarily by the state at universities and research institutions. Because of war-related losses in human and institutional resources, research in a number of disciplines was slow in regaining the levels set by international standards.

Reestablished after the war under Allied influence, the educational system of the Federal Republic has been considerably reformed since the mid-1960s. Primary goals of this reform were the facilitation of access to institutions of higher learning and the modernization of curricula with a view to equal opportunity and to the needs of society as a whole. Simultaneously, the older universities were considerably expanded and many new ones established.

After the war, economic reconstruction and the development of stable political institutions were of primary concern. Self-satisfaction following the successful achievement of these goals has been increasingly challenged since the mid-sixties by criticism of social and political conditions and prevailing values. This criticism has to a certain extent shaken the traditional authority of officialdom. In the name of emancipation, it has led to more extensive participation in many areas. It has also contributed, however, to tensions between generations, between the sexes, in training programs, in schools, and at the universities. Unintended consequences have resulted above all from the extension of bureaucratic areas of authority. In connection with political transition (the beginning of the coalition of the Social Democrats and the Liberals in 1969, the economic recession, and foreign tensions), the change of intellectual climate has made it more difficult to maintain the fundamental social and political consensus in the Federal Republic.

Problems and Issues:

- The position and function of the churches in public life: the dominant role of the two major churches (Roman Catholic and Protestant), and their influence in the area of public affairs and politics; the importance of their social and charitable programs, and their influence on the educational system; moderation of tensions between the confessions through the ecumenical movement
- Strengthening of cultural and scholarly ties to other countries through the Western Allies, through "America Houses", the "Bridge", the Franco-German Youth Alliance, and exchange programs for high school and university students as well as scholars
- The freedom of the arts and sciences constitutionally guaranteed in the Basic Law; substantial government subsidies; "cultural federalism", i.e. state rather than federal autonomy in cultural affairs
- Increase in the number of students qualifying for admission to institutions of higher learning from approximately one in twenty to one in four or five in a generation (ca. 5 percent in 1950, ca. 20–25 percent in 1980); the challenge of relating the education and training system to the job market

- Nachkriegs- und Gegenwartsarchitektur als Folge, Ausdruck und Faktor sozialer, ökonomischer und mentaler Veränderungen in der Gesellschaft
- Zusammenhang des Wandels der Mentalität (Zeitgeist) mit Bürgerinitiativen und Protestbewegungen
- veränderte Sozialformen (Jugendkultur und Familie)
- Auseinandersetzung um die Schuldfrage (vor allem hinsichtlich der Kriegsverbrechen, der Verfolgung und Vernichtung von Juden, Zigeunern und anderen Minderheiten, der Verfolgung der innerdeutschen Opposition), Bemühungen um Wiedergutmachung

- Postwar and contemporary architecture as consequence, statement, and factor in social, economic, intellectual, and cultural changes in society
- The connection between the transformation in the climate of opinion (or Zeitgeist) and citizen initiatives and protest movements
- Changed life styles (youth culture and the family)
- Debate on the question of guilt (especially concerning war crimes, the persecution and extermination of Jews, Gypsies, and other minorities, and the persecution of the opposition within Germany); efforts at restitution

II. Die Bundesrepublik Deutschland im internationalen Zusammenhang

Bei der Erörterung der außenpolitischen Verbindungen der Bundesrepublik Deutschland sind folgende allgemeine Aspekte wichtig:

a) Das westliche Sicherheitssystem

Die grundlegende außenpolitische Entscheidung der Bundesrepublik war die „Westorientierung", in deren Folge sich die Bundesrepublik Deutschland dem westlichen Sicherheits- und Wirtschaftssystem eingliederte, ohne daß dabei das Ziel der Wiedervereinigung aufgegeben wurde. Dadurch entstand ein Zielkonflikt, der bis heute existiert. Als Mitglied der NATO (seit 1955) leistet die Bundesrepublik politisch und militärisch einen erheblichen Beitrag zum atlantischen Bündnis. Gleichzeitig hat sie auf die Produktion von Atomwaffen verzichtet. Ihre Bundeswehr ist in ihrer Gesamtheit der NATO unterstellt. Die Sicherheit der Bundesrepublik wird durch die Verteidigungsgarantie der westlichen Bündnispartner, die sich auch auf die Berliner Westsektoren erstreckt, gewährleistet.

Themen und Probleme:

- Deutschland und der „Kalte Krieg"
- Bedeutung der „Westorientierung": Entscheidung gegen außenpolitische Alternativen (Neutralitätskonzept) und Inkaufnahme der Verfestigung der deutschen Teilung („Freiheit vor Einheit"), obwohl die Teilung weder von der Bundesregierung noch von den großen Parteien offiziell akzeptiert ist**
- Überwindung nationalstaatlicher Konzepte der SPD und der innenpolitischen Widerstände gegen die Aufrüstung der Bundesrepublik durch die Politik Adenauers
- Wiederbewaffnung (Konzept des „Staatsbürgers in Uniform"; „ohne mich"-Bewegung; Recht auf Kriegsdienstverweigerung aus Gewissensgründen; Ersatzdienst)

b) Europäische Integration

Die internationale Stellung der Bundesrepublik ist wesentlich bestimmt durch ihre wirtschaftliche, rechtliche, kulturelle und politische Einbindung in übernationale westeuropäische Zusammenschlüsse. Als Mitglied der EG und des Europa-Rates hat die Bundesrepublik Verpflichtungen und Verantwortung im westeuropäischen Rahmen übernommen.

Die Aufnahme in die westeuropäische Gemeinschaft war Voraussetzung und Folge der Versöhnung mit den westlichen Nachbarstaaten der Bundesrepublik, insbesondere mit Frankreich. Nicht zuletzt dadurch konnte die Bundesrepublik ihre politische und völkerrechtliche Isolierung der Nachkriegszeit überwinden und die Wiederherstellung ihrer Souveränität erreichen.

Themen und Probleme:

- Übernahme der Haftung für Kriegsfolgeschäden durch die Bundesrepublik („Wiedergutmachung")
- Einsatz der Bundesrepublik für die Aufnahme neuer Mitglieder in die EG (insbesondere Englands)
- bedeutender finanzieller Beitrag der Bundesrepublik zum Haushalt der EG

** Vgl. Nachwort des Herausgebers zur dritten Auflage.

II. The International Relations of the Federal Republic of Germany

With respect to the foreign relations of the Federal Republic of Germany the following general considerations are important:

a) The Western Security System

The fundamental foreign policy decision of the Federal Republic of Germany was to turn toward the West. As a consequence, it joined the Western economic and security systems without, however, giving up its basic commitment to German unity. This dichotomy resulted in a conflict of goals which still exists. As a member of NATO since 1955, the Federal Republic makes a substantial political and military contribution to the Atlantic alliance. At the same time, it has foregone the production of atomic weapons. The German Armed Forces are under NATO command. The security of the Federal Republik is guaranteed by the Western allies under the terms of an agreement that also covers the Western sectors of Berlin.

Problems and Issues:

- Germany and the Cold War
- The significance of the decision for orientation toward the West: rejection of alternatives (such as neutrality) and resignation to the deepening division of Germany (giving freedom priority over unity), although the division is not officially accepted by the government or the major political parties
- Adenauer's policies of overcoming the nation state concepts of the Social Democratic Party and domestic political opposition to rearmament in the Federal Republic
- Rearmament (concept of the citizen soldier; the "count-me-out" movement; the right of conscientious objection to military service; alternative service)

b) European Integration

The international position of the Federal Republic of Germany is essentially determined by its economic, legal, cultural, and political integration into transnational West European institutions. As a member of the European Community and the Council of Europe, the Federal Republic has assumed obligations and responsibilities on a West European scale.

The integration of the Federal Republic into the West European community was both a precondition for and the result of its reconciliation with its western neighboring states, particularly France. This was a major factor in enabling the Federal Republic to overcome the international legal and political isolation of the postwar period and to achieve the restoration of its sovereignty.

Problems and Issues:

- Assumption by the Federal Republic of liability for war-related damages (restitution)
- Role of the Federal Republic in supporting the admission of new members, particularly Great Britain, into the European Community
- Significant financial contribution of the Federal Republic to the European Community budget

c) *Ost-West-Beziehungen*

Als geteiltes Land stand Deutschland in den fünfziger Jahren im Mittelpunkt der durch den Kalten Krieg gekennzeichneten Ost-West-Beziehungen. Die Wiederherstellung der nationalen Einheit („Deutsche Frage") wurde durch den Ost-West-Konflikt verhindert. Auch angesichts der geographischen Lage, der Größe, des wirtschaftlichen Potentials Deutschlands und der unterschiedlichen Interessen beider Seiten war die Entlassung der deutschen Staaten aus dem jeweiligen Blocksystem und ihre Wiedervereinigung kaum denkbar; dabei spielten die Interpretationen historischer Erfahrungen eine Rolle.

Die Veränderung der außen- und innenpolitischen Rahmenbedingungen in den sechziger Jahren, darunter auch die neue Westpolitik der osteuropäischen Staaten, veranlaßte die Regierung der Bundesrepublik (Kabinett Brandt/Scheel) nach Konsultation mit den Westmächten zu einer neuen Ostpolitik. Deren Ergebnisse waren Verträge mit der Sowjetunion, der Volksrepublik Polen, der CSSR und der DDR** (und das Vier-Mächte-Abkommen über Berlin), die unter dem Vorbehalt eines künftigen Friedensvertrages den Status quo in Ost- und Mitteleuropa als Grundlage der politischen Beziehungen anerkannten. Diese Politik der Entspannung machte die multilateralen Vereinbarungen der KSZE zur Konfliktregelung in Europa und den Beitritt der beiden deutschen Staaten zur UNO möglich.

Themen und Probleme:

- besondere Bedeutung des Vertrages mit der Volksrepublik Polen: Anerkennung der Westgrenze Polens durch die Bundesrepublik Deutschland**; materielle Wiedergutmachung an die Volksrepublik Polen; Erleichterung der Ausreise von Personen deutscher Abstammung aus Polen
- Politik der Aussöhnung mit den Völkern Osteuropas

d) *Die Beziehung der Bundesrepublik Deutschland zu außereuropäischen Staaten*

Die Bundesrepublik hatte in den ersten Jahren ihres Bestehens diplomatische Beziehungen nur zu solchen Staaten unterhalten, die ihren aus der Rechtsnachfolge des Deutschen Reiches abgeleiteten Alleinvertretungs-Anspruch respektierten und also die DDR nicht anerkannten (sog. Hallstein-Doktrin, 1955). Dieses Prinzip, das sich gegen die Legitimität der DDR richtete, hatte eine Begrenzung des außenpolitischen Handlungsspielraums der Bundesrepublik Deutschland zur Folge. Es wurde im Zuge der Entspannungspolitik schrittweise aufgegeben, um die außenpolitischen Interessen der Bundesrepublik Deutschland der veränderten Lage anzupassen.

Wie die meisten westlichen Industrieländer leistet die Bundesrepublik einen Beitrag zur Entwicklungshilfe, den sie seit den sechziger Jahren stärker an den Bedürfnissen der Empfängerländer als an den unmittelbaren Eigeninteressen orientiert. Damit übernahm sie ein größeres Maß von Verantwortung als zuvor im Rahmen der Bemühungen, den Nord-Süd-Konflikt zwischen Industrie- und Entwicklungsländern zu entschärfen.

Die Verfolgung der Juden und der Holocaust während der Zeit des Nationalsozialismus bedingten das besondere Verhältnis der Bundesrepublik zum Staate Israel. Der Aufnahme diplomatischer Beziehungen (1965) zwischen der Bundesrepublik und Israel ging umfangreiche materielle Unterstützung Israels voran, deren rechtliche und moralische Grundlage der Wille zur Wiedergutmachung war. Die historische Schuld des nationalsozialistischen Deutschland gegenüber den Juden ist vor allem in den Bildungseinrichtungen und Massen-

** Vgl. Nachwort des Herausgebers zur dritten Auflage.

c) East-West Relations

As a divided country, Germany was, in the 1950s, a focal point of the Cold War between East and West. This conflict precluded the restoration of national unity (the "German question"). Considering Germany's geographic location, its size, its economic potential, and the different interests of the two sides in the East-West conflict, it was hardly conceivable that the two German states would separate from their respective bloc systems and achieve reunification. This was a question in which the interpretation of history played a role.

The domestic and foreign changes in the 1960s, including new policies toward the West on the part of Eastern European states, caused the Federal Republic of Germany (under the Brandt-Scheel cabinet, 1969–1974), in consultation with the Western powers, to initiate a new policy toward the East. It resulted in treaties with the Soviet Union, Poland, Czechoslovakia, and the German Democratic Republic under which the status quo in Eastern and Central Europe was recognized as a basis for political relations, subject to the provisions of a future peace treaty for Germany as a whole.

The Federal Republic's policy of détente with the East (the so-called Ostpolitik) was intimately linked with multilateral arrangements that would hardly have been possible without them: the Helsinki Accords (CSCE), the Four-Power Agreement on Berlin, and the admission by the United Nations of both German states to full membership.

Problems and Issues:

- Special importance of the treaty with Poland: recognition of Poland's western boundary by the Federal Republic of Germany; material restitution to the Polish People's Republic; easing of Polish emigration restrictions for ethnic Germans
- Policy of reconciliation with the peoples of Eastern Europe

d) The Relations of the Federal Republic of Germany with Non-European States

In the first years of its existence, the Federal Republic maintained diplomatic relations only with those states which recognized its claim to being the legal successor to the German Reich and therefore the only German state entitled to recognition and which, therefore, did not recognize the GDR (the so-called Hallstein Doctrine of 1955). This policy, which denied the legitimacy of the German Democratic Republic, limited the Federal Republic's flexibility in the conduct of foreign affairs. In the course of détente, one exception to the Hallstein Doctrine after another was negotiated, and it was finally abandoned altogether, in order to enable the Federal Republic to represent its interests in a changed situation.

Like most Western industrialized countries, the Federal Republic contributes to development aid; since the 1960s this aid has been increasingly adapted to the needs of the recipient countries instead of serving the immediate interests of the Federal Republic. Thereby the Federal Republic thas assumed a greater measure of responsibility than before in the effort to ameliorate the North-South conflict between industrialized an developing countries.

The persecution of the Jews and the Holocaust during the National Socialist period postulate the special relationship between the Federal Republic and the State of Israel. The assumption of diplomatic relations between the two countries in 1965 was preceded by extensive material assistance. The legal and moral basis for this was the desire to make

medien der Bundesrepublik Deutschland nachhaltig verdeutlicht worden. Antisemitische Äußerungen und Aktivitäten werden von den politisch Verantwortlichen und der breiten Öffentlichkeit der Bundesrepublik verurteilt.

Themen und Probleme:

- die Höhe des Entwicklungsbeitrages der Bundesrepublik; international vereinbarte Norm (0,7 % des Bruttosozialprodukts); Vergleich mit einigen anderen Industriestaaten
- Wiedergutmachungs-Vertrag zwischen der Bundesrepublik und Israel vom 10. 9. 1952
- Abkommen zwischen Adenauer und Ben Gurion über Waffenlieferungen (1960)
- Belastung des Verhältnisses zu Israel durch die ungelöste Palästinenserfrage und die Politisierung deutsch-arabischer Wirtschaftsbeziehungen (Politik der Europäischen Gemeinschaft)
- Kriegsverbrecher-Prozesse und nationalsozialistische Gewaltverbrechens-Prozesse*

* Vgl. Anmerkung auf S. 10

restitution. The historic guilt of National Socialist Germany toward the Jews has been persistently emphasized, especially in the educational institutions and the mass media of the Federal Republic of Germany. Anti-Semitic expressions and activities are condemned by the authorities and the general public in the Federal Republic of Germany.

Problems and Issues:

- The level of development assistance by the Federal Republic; the internationally agreed standard (0.7 % of GNP); comparison with some other industrialized states
- Restitution Treaty between the Federal Republic of Germany and Israel of 10 September 1952
- Agreement between Adenauer and Ben Gurion on the supply of weapons (1960)
- Complication of the relationship with Israel by the unresolved problem of the Palestinians and by the politicization of German-Arab economic relations (the policy of the European Community)
- Trials for war crimes and National Socialist atrocities*

---

* See note on p. 11

III. Das Verhältnis der Bundesrepublik Deutschland zur Deutschen Demokratischen Republik

Deutsche Geschichte nach dem Zweiten Weltkrieg ist als Konsequenz der Teilung Deutschlands und Europas vornehmlich die Geschichte zweier deutscher Staaten. Die Bundesrepublik Deutschland betrachtet die Beziehungen zur DDR nicht als außenpolitische Beziehungen, sondern als „Beziehungen besonderer Art".

Seit 1946 erzwang die Sozialistische Einheitspartei Deutschlands (SED), gestützt auf die sowjetische Besatzungsmacht, den Aufbau eines kommunistischen Systems. Durch Demontage, eine erhebliche Reparationslast, ständige Entnahme aus der laufenden Produktion durch die UdSSR und durch das sowjetische Verbot, die Marshallplanhilfe anzunehmen, verzögerte sich im Vergleich zur Bundesrepublik der wirtschaftliche Aufschwung der DDR. Hinzu trat eine Massenflucht der Bevölkerung in die Bundesrepublik, deren Ursachen die Einschränkung der persönlichen Freiheit durch politische Reglementierung in der DDR sowie das Wohlstandsgefälle zwischen beiden deutschen Staaten war. Um die dadurch entstehenden politischen und ökonomischen Probleme zu beheben, schloß die DDR die Grenze zur Bundesrepublik hermetisch ab; aber erst durch den Bau der Mauer in Berlin (1961) wurde die Massenflucht unterbunden.

Die DDR verfolgte im ersten Jahrzehnt ihres Bestehens im engen Bündnis mit der Sowjetunion eine Politik der Wiederherstellung der Einheit Deutschlands nach kommunistischem Muster. Nach einer Phase innerer und äußerer Konsolidierung, verbunden mit dem Aufbau der im Warschauer Pakt integrierten Nationalen Volksarmee, gewann die DDR eine bedeutende Stellung im COMECON als zweitgrößter Industriestaat mit dem höchsten Lebensstandard; als wichtiger militärischer Verbündeter im Warschauer Pakt erreichte sie – auch infolge der Entspannungspolitik – internationale Anerkennung. Seit 1974 vertritt ihre Führung die These, daß zwei verschiedene Nationen auf deutschem Boden existieren: eine „sozialistische" und eine „kapitalistische" Nation. Der Zielkonflikt zwischen der Bundesrepublik und der DDR hinsichtlich der künftigen Gestaltung Deutschlands ist durch politische, wirtschaftliche und humanitäre Regelungen in den siebziger Jahren und durch das Berlin-Abkommen der vier Mächte (1971) zwar gemildert, aber nicht beigelegt worden. Nach wie vor bleibt die „Deutsche Frage" Teil des weltpolitischen Gegensatzes.

Themen und Probleme:

- Sonderkonflikt zwischen beiden deutschen Staaten (unter Einschluß Berlins) als Teil des Ost-West-Konflikts (u.a. Frage der Staatsbürgerschaft)
- Überwindung der Widerstände in der SBZ: Zwangsvereinigung von KPD und SPD zur SED, Gleichschaltung bürgerlicher Parteien, Unterordnung der Gewerkschaften unter die Partei, Niederwerfung des Aufstandes vom 17. Juni 1953
- starke Fluchtbewegung in die Bundesrepublik; hermetische Schließung der Grenze zwischen der Bundesrepublik und der DDR
- repressive Reaktion auf Systemkritik, u.a. durch Ausweisung
- Fortbestehen von Beziehungen zwischen beiden deutschen Staaten durch Empfang der Mediensendungen, Besucherverkehr und Familienbegegnungen, sowie durch zollfreien Handel, wodurch die DDR wirtschaftliche Vorteile aus der Mitgliedschaft der Bundesrepublik in der EG genießt

III. The Relationship of the Federal Republic of Germany to the German Democratic Republic

German history since World War II is, as a consequence of the division of Germany and Europe, primarily the history of two German states. The Federal Republic of Germany does not consider its relations with the German Democratic Republic to be foreign relations in the conventional sense, but a "special relationship".

Beginning in 1946, the Socialist Unity Party of Germany (SED), with the support of Soviet occupation authorities, forced the establishement of a Communist system in the Soviet zone of occupation. Dismantlements, a considerable reparations burden, the steady syphoning off of current production by the USSR, and the Soviet prohibition against the acceptance of Marshall Plan aid delayed the economic recovery of the GDR in comparison to the Federal Republic. In addition, there was a mass population flight into the Federal Republic, the causes of which included limitations on individual freedom by political regimentation, and the difference in the standard of living between the two German states. To remedy the resultant political and economic consequences, the GDR hermetically sealed its border with the Federal Republic. The steady drain of human resources was not ended until 1961, however, when the Berlin Wall was constructed to close the last avenue of escape.

In the first decade of its existence, the GDR, in close coordination with the Soviet Union, pursued a policy seeking the reunification of Germany along Communist lines. A period of domestic and foreign consolidation was accompanied by the development of a national army and its integration into the Warsaw Pact. The GDR attained an important position in COMECON as its second largest industrial state, and the one with the highest standard of living. Already an important ally in the Warsaw Pact, it gained – in part as a result of the general détente – international recognition.

Since 1974, the leaders of the GDR have advocated the thesis that two separate nations exist on German soil: a "socialist" nation and a "capitalist" nation. The tension between the Federal Republic of Germany and the GDR regarding the difference in aims for the future of Germany has been ameliorated by the Four-Power Berlin Agreement of 1971 and by the political, economic, and humanitarian arrangements of the 1970s, but it has not been removed. The "German Question" remains, as much as ever, one of the world's unresolved political issues.

Problems and Issues:

- The special conflict between the two German states (with consideration of Berlin) as an aspect of the East-West conflict (taking into account, among other things, the question of German citizenship)
- Overcoming the opposition in the Soviet Zone of Germany: the compulsory unification of the German Communist party and the Social Democratic party in the new Socialist Unity party; the abolition of independence of the middle-class parties; the subordination of the trade unions to the party; the suppression of the revolt of 17 June 1953
- Mass flight to the Federal Republic; the hermetic sealing of the border between the Federal Republic and the GDR
- Repressive reaction against any criticism of the regime by means such as expulsion
- Continuation of relations between the two German states through receipt of broadcasts, family reunions and travel by visitors, as well as duty-free trade (affording the GDR economic advantages because of the Federal Republic's membership in the European Community)

IV. Das Verhältnis zwischen der Bundesrepublik Deutschland und den Vereinigten Staaten

Die Beziehungen zwischen der Bundesrepublik Deutschland und den Vereinigten Staaten haben besondere Bedeutung.

Das Verhältnis zwischen der Bundesrepublik und den Vereinigten Staaten beruht nicht nur auf vielen gemeinsamen Interessen, sondern auch auf einem weitgehenden Grundkonsens über demokratische Wertvorstellungen. Der amerikanische Einfluß in Wissenschaft, Technologie, Kultur und im Alltagsleben seit Ende des Krieges und der wachsende Austausch zwischen beiden Ländern haben diesen Prozeß noch verstärkt. Überdies kam es zu einer engen wirtschaftlichen Verflechtung – z.B. durch multinationale Konzerne und Kapitalinvestitionen –, die neben Kooperation auch Konflikte verursachten.

In den ersten Jahren ihres Bestehens befand sich die Bundesrepublik in politischer und militärischer Abhängigkeit von den Vereinigten Staaten und war auf deren wirtschaftliche Hilfe angewiesen. Während die Bundesrepublik im Sicherheitsbereich, auch nach dem Aufbau konventioneller Streitkräfte, vom Schutz vor allem durch die USA abhängig blieb, bildete sich im politischen und wirtschaftlichen Bereich ein stärker partnerschaftliches Verhältnis aus.

Auch die unterschiedlichen Rollen (USA als Globalmacht, die Bundesrepublik Deutschland als regionale Macht im Zusammenhang der Europäischen Gemeinschaft) und innenpolitische Unterschiede ließen wiederholt Differenzen über politische und wirtschaftliche Ziele und Methoden entstehen. In der Geschichte der deutsch-amerikanischen Beziehungen hat es jedoch nie ein so enges Verhältnis gegeben wie das zwischen der Bundesrepublik Deutschland und den USA. Dieses muß ungeachtet der auf beiden Seiten sich von Zeit zu Zeit äußernden Kritik und mancher ernsthafter Besorgnisse über die jeweilige Politik betont werden. Dennoch ist die Kenntnis des jeweiligen anderen Landes unzulänglich geblieben. Stereotype Vorstellungen und Urteile sind beiderseitig weit verbreitet. Gleichwohl besteht eine weithin positive Einstellung der Bevölkerung zu den Vereinigten Staaten und ein Bewußtsein von Gemeinsamkeiten der Überzeugungen, Lebensformen und vitalen politischen Interessen.

Themen und Probleme:

- die Wende der amerikanischen Besatzungspolitik 1947/48; Wirtschaftshilfe, Care-Pakete, kirchliche Hilfen und die Berliner Luftbrücke als Beginn eines deutsch-amerikanischen Vertrauensverhältnisses
- US-Truppen in der Bundesrepublik: von der Besatzungsmacht über die Schutzmacht zum Verbündeten
- wirtschaftliche Verflechtungen, u.a. durch multinationale Konzerne, gegenseitige Kapitalinvestitionen
- Rezeption amerikanischer Forschung und Technologie (z.B. in der Biologie, Psychologie, in den Sozialwissenschaften, in der Computertechnik und Elektronik); Konsumgewohnheiten; Ankauf von Fernsehserien; Rezeption von Kunst- und Kulturströmungen: Jazz, Pop-Art, Popmusik, Protestsongs in der Bundesrepublik
- unterschiedliche Vorstellung in der Währungspolitik; Konsultationsprobleme im Atlantischen Bündnis; Konflikte politischer und wirtschaftlicher Interessen im Osthandel
- Wirkungen von stereotypen Vorstellungen über Deutschland und die Deutschen in Kriegs- und Nazifilmen; Zuschreibung negativer Züge zum „deutschen Charakter"; das Bild des „ugly American" als „rücksichtlos und unkultiviert"
- antiamerikanische Manifestationen anläßlich des Vietnamkrieges; Proteste gegen Raketenstationierung, Rassendiskriminierung; Gemeinsamkeiten zwischen amerikanischen und deutschen Protestbewegungen
- Umwelt- und Verbraucherschutz als Beispiele gegenseitiger Anregung und Zusammenarbeit

IV. The Relationship Between the Federal Republic of Germany and the United States of America

The relationship between the Federal Republic of Germany and the United States is of special importance for both countries.

This relationship is based not only on many common interests, but also on a far-reaching, commonly held consensus about democratic values. American influence in science, technology, culture, and everyday life since the end of the war, and the growing exchange between the two countries have strengthened this consensus. In addition, close economic ties have developed, in part through multinational enterprises and capital investments, which have brought controversy as well as cooperation.

During the first years after its establishment, the Federal Republic was politically and militarily dependent on the United States and required its economic assistance. Even after the development of its own conventional armed forces, the Federal Republic continued to depend primarily on the USA for its protection; in the political and economic sphere a relationship emerged that was much more of a partnership.

The different roles of the two countries (the United States as a global power, the Federal Republic as a regional power linked to the European Community) and differences in their domestic politics have repeatedly led to disagreements between them regarding political and economic methods and goals. In the history of German-American relations there has nonetheless never been so close a relationship as that between the Federal Republic and the United States. This must be stressed despite the fact that periodically one hears in each country criticism and expressions of serious concern regarding the other's policy at the time.

In each country there is inadequate knowledge of the other. In both, images and judgments based largely on stereotypes abound. Be that as it may, the people of the Federal Republic have a generally positive attitude toward the United States and a conscious awareness of common convictions, life styles, and vital political interests.

Problems and Issues:

- The turning point in American occupation policy (1947–48); CARE packages, aid through the churches, economic assistance, and the Berlin Airlift as the beginning of a German-American relationship of mutual trust
- U.S. Forces in the Federal Republic: the transition from occupation to protection to alliance
- Economic interpenetration, inter alia through multinational enterprises and mutual capital investments
- Reception of American research and technology (e.g., in biology, psychology, the social sciences, computer technology, and electronics); consumerism: purchases of television series; adoption in the Federal Republic of American trends in culture and the arts: jazz, pop art, pop music, and protest songs
- Differing approaches to monetary policy; problems of consultation in the Atlantic Alliance; conflicts between political and economic interests in trade with the Eastern bloc
- Effect of stereotyped images of Germany and the Germans in motion pictures on the National Socialist period and the war; the attribution of negative traits to the "German character"; the image of the "ugly American" as "inconsiderate and uncultivated"
- Anti-American manifestations during the war in Vietnam; protests in Germany against the basing of missiles in the Federal Republic and against racial discrimination in America; similarities between American and German protest movements
- Protection of the environment and of the consumer as examples of mutual encouragement and collaboration

B. Empfehlungen zur Behandlung der US-amerikanischen Geschichte seit 1945

In der Zeit zwischen 1945 und 1980 haben sich entscheidende Wandlungen in Gesellschaft und Außenpolitik der Vereinigten Staaten vollzogen. Zum Teil durch den Zweiten Weltkrieg verursacht, der ein Katalysator für eine Reihe folgenreicher Entwicklungen war, haben die Vereinigten Staaten einen ausgedehnten Wohlfahrtsstaat geschaffen und sind in ihrer Rolle als Weltmacht Verpflichtungen in einem zuvor ungekannten Ausmaß eingegangen. Obgleich starke Kräfte darauf abzielten, dauerhafte, historisch verfestigte soziale Trennlinien regionaler, rassischer und ethnischer Art zu überwinden, bleiben die USA weiterhin ein Land mit beträchtlichen inneren Unterschieden. Beim Versuch, allgemeine Aussagen über die amerikanische Gesellschaft zu machen, sollte man sich stets vergegenwärtigen, daß die Vereinigten Staaten eine riesige, pluralistische Nation geblieben sind.

I. Staat und Gesellschaft

a) Demographische und wirtschaftliche Entwicklungen

Zwischen 1945 und 1980 haben, zum Teil durch die sozialen und ökonomischen Folgen des Zweiten Weltkrieges bedingt, wichtige demographische Wandlungen stattgefunden. Eine davon war der „Babyboom“ zwischen 1940 und 1965, der einen wesentlichen Anteil an der Verdoppelung der Bevölkerung hat. Zu anderen wichtigen Veränderungen in dieser Zeit gehört die legale Einwanderung von ca. 10 Millionen Menschen sowie die rapide anwachsende illegale Einwanderung vor allem aus Mexiko. Im Jahre 1965 wurde das System nationaler Quoten von 1924, das die Einwanderung von Westeuropäern begünstigt hatte, abgeschafft. Die Binnenwanderung vom Nordosten zum „Sonnengürtel“ im Süden und Südwesten des Landes verstärkte sich in dieser Periode stetig, während der Zug der Schwarzen und der armen Weißen in die großen Städte des Nordens zwischen 1940 und den frühen 60er Jahren dramatisch anschwoll, sich dann mit gedrosseltem Tempo fortsetzte. Wegen der beträchtlichen Verringerung der in der Landwirtschaft tätigen bäuerlichen Bevölkerung und wegen des Wegzugs aus den kleinen Städten entwickelte die Bevölkerung einen mehr und mehr städtischen und vorstädtischen Charakter.

Das Bruttosozialprodukt wies steile Steigerungsraten auf und trug zum schnellen Anwachsen der Mittelschichten (gleichgültig, ob durch Beruf oder Einkommen definiert) ebenso bei wie zur deutlichen Verbesserung des materiellen Lebensstandards. Einige der Gründe für dieses Wachstum waren die Intensivierung der Landwirtschaft und die Entwicklung neuer Technologien (Computer, Automatisierung, Raumfahrt, Nachrichtentechnologien).

Obgleich ältere Probleme wie Arbeitslosigkeit und Inseln von Armut überdauerten, und obwohl Inflation, Energiekrise und die Verlangsamung des Wirtschaftswachstums zu neuen Problemen in den 70er Jahren führten, bleibt der enorme materielle Fortschritt die hervorstechende Tatsache im amerikanischen Wirtschaftsleben der Nachkriegszeit.

b) Soziokulturelle Entwicklungen und Politikbereiche

Seit dem Ende des Zweiten Weltkrieges haben weitreichende soziale Wandlungen in den Vereinigten Staaten stattgefunden. Wichtige Trends waren: rapider Verfall in einigen der älteren Städte im Nordosten und mittleren Westen, den man in einigen Städten durch aktive städtepolitische Maßnahmen aufzuhalten versuchte; Herausbildung von Vorstädten mit eigenen, in sich unterschiedlichen soziokulturellen Strukturen („suburbia“); Zusammenwachsen der großen Städte („megalopolis“); sowie eine Konzentration von Schwarzen und spanischsprachigen Amerikanern in den Zentren vieler Städte.

B. Recommendations Concerning the Treatment of U.S. History since 1945

The period 1945–1980 witnessed great changes in American society and foreign relations. In part because of World War II, which was a catalyst for many significant developments, the United States created an expanded welfare state and accepted unprecedented commitments in its role as a world power. Despite forces that challenged historically durable social divisions – regional, racial, ethnic – considerable variations persist in America. In seeking to generalize concerning American life since 1945, it is essential to remember that the United States remains a vast, pluralistic nation.

I. State and Society

a) Demographic and Economic Developments

Many important demographic changes took place between 1945 and 1980, in part because of the social and economic impact of World War II. One was a baby boom between 1940 and 1965, which contributed greatly to a two-fold increase in the population. Other important changes during the period included legal immigration amounting to about ten million (marked in 1965 by the abolition of the nationality quota system of 1924 which had been favorable to West Europeans), and illegal immigration, especially from Mexico, showing a marked increase. The domestic population movement, from the Northeast to the Sun Belt of the South and Southwest, increased steadily during this period, while the movement of blacks and poor whites into the major population centers of the North increased dramatically between 1940 and the early 1960's and then continued at a slower rate. Owing to a substantial decline in the number of farmers and to movements of people out of small towns, the population became steadily more urban and suburban.

The gross national product grew at an amazing pace, contributing to a swift growth in the middle classes (whether defined by occupation or income) and to a substantial improvement in the material standards of living. Among the reasons for this growth were the following: intensification of agriculture, and development of new technologies (computers, automation, astronautics, communications technologies).

Although old problems, such as unemployment and pockets of poverty, persisted, and though inflation, the "energy crisis", and a slowing of growth created new difficulties in the 1970's, the pre-eminent fact of postwar economic life in America has been striking material progress.

b) Socio-Cultural Developments and Policies

Since the end of World War II there have been far-reaching social changes in the United States. Among important trends were the following: accelerated decay in some of the older cities of the Northeast and Midwest, partially relieved in some places by urban renewal; development of suburbs with their own varied socio-cultural structures ("suburbia"); development of extensive urban sprawl ("megalopolis"); and concentration of blacks and Hispanic Americans in core areas of many cities.

Das Familienleben und die Lebensformen bestimmter Gruppen waren beträchtlichem Wandel unterworfen. Unter diese Wandlungen fallen z. B. die steil ansteigende Scheidungsrate, die Gefahr einer Entfremdung zwischen den Generationen besonders in der oberen Mittelschicht, sowie ein rapides Anwachsen der außerhäuslichen Berufstätigkeit von Frauen. In einigen Bereichen der amerikanischen Gesellschaft entwickelten sich nach 1960 eine neue Jugendkultur und Experimente mit neuen Formen des Zusammenlebens. Vordergründig waren diese Bewegungen durch einen radikalen Bruch mit Mode, Haartracht und musikalischem Geschmack gekennzeichnet; hinter diesem Bruch mit äußeren Konventionen verbargen sich jedoch bei einigen dieser Gruppen starke Überzeugungen im Hinblick auf sexuelle Freizügigkeit, Religiosität, pazifistische Werte und soziale Revolution. Von den Überzeugungen der meisten älteren Amerikaner unterschieden sich diese neuen Werthaltungen scharf.

In der gleichen Zeitspanne war ein außerordentlich großer Zuwachs von jungen Amerikanern zu beobachten, die die High School absolvierten und die Colleges und Universitäten besuchten (in den 70er Jahren traten über 50 % eines Jahrgangs in weiterführende Bildungsinstitutionen ein). Während einige dieser Colleges und Universitäten unter dem Ansturm der Studenten ihre Ausbildungsstandards senkten, florierten andere und förderten (insbesondere in den medizinischen und naturwissenschaftlichen Fächern) die Forschung, die weltweite Bedeutung erlangte. Auch viele ältere Amerikaner nutzten das breite Angebot technischer und anderer, speziell auf die Erwachsenenbildung ausgerichteter Kurse. Teilweise durch Regierungssubventionen für die Schönen Künste gefördert, entstanden viele neue Museen, Orchester und Theatergruppen. Das Fernsehen, sowohl die kommerziellen wie die öffentlichen Programme, erreichte mit seinem Angebot bereits 1960 nahezu jeden amerikanischen Haushalt und trug zur Entwicklung einer breiten Volkskultur bei.

Im Zuge des sich rasant entwickelnden Wohlfahrtsstaates wurde besonders in den 60er Jahren eine Anzahl wichtiger neuer Programme durchgeführt, mit denen beachtliche, aber nicht hinreichende Erfolge erzielt wurden. Dazu gehören: die Ausweitung des Anspruchs auf Sozialhilfe („social security") auf bislang nicht berechtigte Gruppen, enorme Zuwächse der Sozialhilfeleistungen, die Einführung einer Krankenversicherung für nicht mehr im Arbeitsprozeß stehende ältere Bürger (Medicare) und eine Krankenversicherung für Wohlfahrtsempfänger (Medicaid), eine Erweiterung der Berechtigung für den Bezug von Lebensmittelmarken sowie eine Liberalisierung des Anspruchs auf den Empfang von Wohlfahrtsunterstützung. Zum ersten Mal in der amerikanischen Geschichte sorgte die Bundesregierung nach 1945 für groß angelegte Ausbildungsprogramme für Veteranen, förderte die elementare und weiterführende Erziehung und unterstützte auf unterschiedliche Weise Wissenschaftler und Studenten der Colleges und Universitäten. Versuche einer aktiven Umweltpolitik wurden ebenfalls unternommen. Viele soziale Probleme blieben ungelöst, andere entstanden neu und konnten weder auf bundes- noch auf einzelstaatlicher Ebene gelöst werden. Dazu gehören der allgemein angenommene Anstieg von Kriminalität und von Gewalttätigkeit sowie der Verfall der allgemeinen Lebensqualität.

c) *Bürgerrechte*

Keine der inneren Entwicklungen im Amerika der Nachkriegszeit hatte stärkere Auswirkungen und verlief dramatischer als die Bürgerrechtsbewegung. Viele Kräfte trugen zu dieser Bewegung bei: die Erfahrungen schwarzer Soldaten im II. Weltkrieg; der wachsende Wohlstand der Nachkriegszeit, der durch die Befriedigung materieller Bedürfnisse dazu beitrug, Amerikaner der Mittelklasse für die Idee der Gleichheit aufgeschlossen zu machen, sowie das Insistieren schwarzer wie weißer Amerikaner auf einer frei von Gesichtspunkten

Patterns of life of families and of various groups changed considerably. Among these changes were a rapidly increasing divorce rate; a possible generation gap, particularly in the upper middle classes; and a substantial growth in the employment of women outside the home. In some sectors of American society there developed after 1960 gropings toward a new youth culture and experiments in communal living. On the surface these were marked by radical departures from conventional dress styles, hair styles, and musical tastes; more fundamentally some of these groups held strong beliefs – in sexual freedom, religious cults, pacifism, and social revolution – which diverged sharply from the beliefs of most older Americans.

The period also witnessed a staggering increase in the percentage and numbers of young Americans who finished high school and attended college and universities (more than 50 % entered institutions of post-secondary education by the 1970's). While some of these colleges and universities had to offer the new masses of students a lower quality of education, others flourished and promoted research (especially in medicine and science) of worldwide significance. Many older Americans also took part in a range of technical courses and adult education classes. Thanks in part to government subsidies to the arts and humanities, many museums, orchestras, and dramatic groups sprang up. Television, with an immense spectrum of offerings by both commercial and public broadcasting, reached all but a few American homes as early as 1960 and contributed to the development of a common popular culture.

As part of a rapidly developing welfare state, important new social programs were introduced, especially in the 1960's, with considerable but not complete success. Among these were: the extension of social security to previously uncovered groups; great increases in social security benefits; Medicare (for older citizens) and Medicaid (for the poor); rapid expansion of the food stamp program; and liberalization of welfare. The federal government, for the first time in American history, provided large-scale educational assistance to veterans, aided elementary and secondary education, and provided various forms of assistance to scholars and college and university students. Efforts were also made at an improvement of the environment. Many social problems continued, and others arose and were not solved by federal and state efforts. Among them were a perceived increase in crime and violence and a decline in the quality of life.

c) *Civil Rights*

No domestic development in postwar America was more dramatic and important than the civil rights movement. Many forces contributed to this movement: the experiences of black soldiers in World War II; the growing postwar affluence which, by helping to satisfy material needs, made middle-class Americans receptive to egalitarian ideas; and the pressure exerted by many Americans, both black and white, for equal justice under law regardless of race. This was pre-eminently a broad social movement which governmental officials were slow to endorse.

der Rassenzugehörigkeit urteilenden Justiz. Die Bürgerrechtsbewegung war in erster Linie eine breite soziale Bewegung, deren Zielen offizielle Regierungsvertreter nur zögernd beipflichteten.

Einige wichtige Ereignisse der Bewegung waren: die Aufhebung der Rassentrennung in der Armee in den späten 40er Jahren; das Urteil des Obersten Gerichtshofs (1954), das die Aufhebung der Rassentrennung in den Schulen verfügte; von Martin Luther King, Jr., und anderen angeführte gewaltlose Demonstrationen und „Freiheitsfahrten", sowie die Gesetzgebung der 60er Jahre, die die Rechtsmäßigkeit der Rassentrennung in allen Bereichen des Alltags aufhob und für den Schutz schwarzer Wähler Sorge trug. Diese Entwicklungen haben Rassenvorurteile und strukturelle Diskriminierungen (etwa die disproportional hohe Arbeitslosigkeit der Schwarzen, ihre Lebensbedingungen in den Slums, ihre geringeren Ausbildungsmöglichkeiten und Erfolgsaussichten, ihre Diskriminierung bei den Beschäftigungschancen) nicht auszulöschen vermocht. Die Bürgerrechtsbewegung spaltete sich Mitte der 60er Jahre („Black-Power"-Bewegung) und bewegte sich mit veränderten Zielen auf die Städte zu. In einigen Städten brachen in den späten 60er Jahren Aufstände aus. Alles in allem haben diese Entwicklungen jedoch den politischen, sozialen und wirtschaftlichen Status schwarzer Amerikaner sowie ihren Bildungsstandard merklich verbessert (vgl. etwa die Wahl von Schwarzen zu Bürgermeistern, selbst in den Städten des Südens; Ernennungen von Schwarzen zu Spitzenpositionen in der Exekutive wie im Justizwesen; einen allgemeinen politischen Machtzuwachs und ein beträchtliches Anwachsen von Schwarzen in der Mittelschicht).

Eine Reihe unvorhergesehener Folgen stellte sich mit dieser Bewegung ein. In dem Maße, in dem immer mehr Amerikaner für Ungleichheit sensibilisiert wurden, entwickelten sich Bewegungen mit dem Ziel, die Rechte anderer schlechter gestellter Gruppen ebenfalls zu erweitern. Das schloß die Älteren („gray power"), ethnische Minderheiten (besonders Indianer und Chicanos), Studenten und, vor allem seit Mitte der 60er Jahre, Frauen ein.

d) Das politische System und seine Krisen

Obgleich es zwischen 1945 und 1980 nur wenige Verfassungsänderungen gegeben hat (Herabsetzung des Wahlalters auf 18 Jahre, Vorsorge für den Fall der Regierungsunfähigkeit des Präsidenten, Begrenzung der Amtszeit des Präsidenten auf zwei Wahlperioden), war das politische System der Vereinigten Staaten in dieser Zeit einer Reihe von Belastungen ausgesetzt, von denen einige eine Zeitlang die politische Struktur selber in Mitleidenschaft zu ziehen drohten. Andere hinterließen Narben. Diese Belastungen sind in der Hauptsache auf interne Reaktionen auf die außenpolitische Rolle der Vereinigten Staaten, auf Konflikte zwischen Exekutive, Legislative und Judikative sowie auf den wachsenden Einfluß von Interessengruppen mit eng definierter Interessenlage zurückzuführen. Das Verhältnis zwischen der Bundesregierung, die ihren Einfluß beträchtlich erweiterte, und den einzelstaatlichen und örtlichen Behörden hat sich in nachhaltiger Weise verändert.

Die Tatsache, daß die Vereinigten Staaten die nichtkommunistische Welt nach dem Zweiten Weltkrieg in einer Konfrontation mit dem sowjetischen Machtblock angeführt haben (vgl. unten II a), ermöglichte es einigen skrupellosen Politikern und Beamten, unterstützt durch eine verbreitete Furcht vor dem Kommunismus, die Gefahr innerer Unterwanderung auszunutzen und die Bürgerrechte zu verletzen. Diese Haltung schlug sich unmißverständlich im Komitee für unamerikanische Umtriebe und in der McCarthy-Ära (1950–1954) nieder. McCarthy selber geriet 1954 in Mißkredit. Aber der Schaden, der Personen und Institutionen zugefügt wurde, war erheblich.

Some of the important events in the movement included: the desegregation of the Armed Forces in the late 1940's; the decision of the Supreme Court (1954) which called for an end to segregated schools; non-violent demonstrations and freedom rides led by Martin Luther King, Jr. and others; and legislation in the 1960's eliminating legal segregation in all aspects of life and providing for the protection of black voters. These developments did not wipe out racial prejudice or institutionalized discrimination (e.g., disproportionate black unemployment, blacks living in slum housing, lower educational opportunities and achievements, discrimination in employment opportunities). Moreover, the civil rights movement split in the mid-1960's ("black power" movement) and moved, with changing goals, to the cities, in some of which riots broke out in the late 1960's. But taken together, these developments greatly improved the political, social, educational, and economic status of American blacks (e.g., election of blacks as mayors, even in Southern cities; black appointments to top government positions in the Executive and Judiciary; general increase in political power; and a considerable growth in the number of blacks in the middle class).

Many unanticipated consequences flowed from this movement. As more Americans became sensitized to inequality, there were popular movements to extend the rights of other deprived groups. These included elderly people ("gray power"), ethnic minorities (particularly Native Americans and Chicanos), student groups, and, especially since the mid-1960's, women.

d) The Political System and its Crises

While there were few federal constitutional changes between 1945 and 1980 (lowering the voting age to eighteen, provision for Presidential disability, limitation of Presidential terms to two), the political system of the United States was subjected to a series of stresses, some of which threatened for a time to affect the structure of government. Others left scars. These stresses in the U.S. were stimulated essentially by several forces: the reaction to the expanded U.S. role in international events, conflicts between the Executive, Legislative and Judicial branches of government, and the growing power of single interest pressure groups. There were also major changes in the relationship between the federal government, which vastly expanded its power, and state and local authorities.

The fact that the United States, after World War II, led the non-Communist world in a confrontation with the Soviet block (see IIa, below), combined with fears of communism, permitted some unscrupulous politicians and officials to exploit the danger of domestic subversion and to violate civil liberties. This attitude manifested itself most broadly in the House Un-American Activities Committee and in McCarthyism (1950–54). McCarthy was discredited by 1954, but great damage was done to individuals and institutions.

Heftige und weitreichende Umwälzungen folgten aus der Ablehnung des Vietnam-Krieges durch einen großen Teil der Bevölkerung. Der Vietnam-Krieg rief eine sich scharf artikulierende Protestbewegung hervor (z. B. Kriegsdienstverweigerer und Protestmärsche). Zwei aufeinanderfolgende Regierungen (Johnson, Nixon) waren außerstande, mit dieser Protestbewegung fertig zu werden. Der Krieg hatte ein tiefes Mißtrauen in die Regierung, vor allem in die Exekutive, zur Folge. Dieses Mißtrauen war besonders bei Studenten im wehrpflichtigen Alter ausgeprägt. Nixons willkürliche Amtsführung, mit der er den Krieg und das Dissenter-Problem handhabte, führte die schwerste politische Krise seit dem Bürgerkrieg herbei: die Watergate-Affäre und den Rücktritt Präsident Nixons 1974, den ersten Rücktritt eines Präsidenten in der Geschichte Amerikas. Die Absichten, von denen Nixon sich hatte leiten lassen, sind nach wie vor heftig umstritten. Die Stärke des politischen Systems (z. B. die Presse, die Autorität des Kongresses, die Stabilität der Justiz, Zivilcourage) hatte sich letztlich bewährt.

Der Vietnam-Krieg und Watergate legten die allmählich vollzogene Machtverschiebung von der Legislative zur Exekutive bloß („die imperiale Präsidentschaft"). Als Reaktion hierauf versuchten Reformer, das durchzusetzen, was ihnen demokratischere Methoden der Kandidatennominierung für politische Ämter zu sein schienen. Bemerkenswert ist die Zunahme von Vorwahlen in den späten 60er Jahren. Das Pendel der Macht schwang während der Regierungen Ford und Carter zum Kongreß zurück. Einige der Reformen waren der War Powers Act [mit der Stärkung der Zuständigkeit des Kongresses für den Einsatz der Streitkräfte], die Zusätze zum Freedom of Information Act und der Privacy Act [durch welche die Regierung zur Offenlegung ihrer Akten verpflichtet ist, gleichzeitig aber persönliche Daten schützen muß], die Errichtung der Budgetbehörde des Kongresses sowie Anstrengungen einer Selbstdisziplinierung, wie sie sich in den Ethics-Committees des Kongresses niederschlugen.

Das Emporkommen von Interessengruppen mit eng umrissener Interessenlage drohte besonders in den 70er Jahren, gelegentlich die Verabschiedung wichtiger Gesetze zu durchkreuzen. Unter den wichtigsten dieser Interessengruppen waren große Konzerne und das Militär. Präsident Eisenhower hatte bereits 1961 vor dem „militärisch-industriellen-Komplex" gewarnt. Vor dem Hintergrund dieser Problematik haben sich Amerikaner in wachsendem Maße an die Gerichte gewandt, um Angelegenheiten, die vormals nicht Sache der Justiz gewesen waren, zu regeln. Viele dieser Fälle gelangten bis zum Obersten Gerichtshof, der unter der Führung von Earl Warren (1953–1969) eine Reihe wichtiger Urteile gefällt hat, die die Rechte von Minoritäten erweiterten, die Rechte von Angeklagten schützten und die dazu führten, daß eine vergleichbare Relation zwischen Wählern und Abgeordneten in den einzelstaatlichen Parlamenten und im nationalen Repräsentantenhaus hergestellt wurde.

Während all dieser Krisen hat sich das politische System als flexibel erwiesen. Seine Stabilität beruht auf einem breiten Konsens im Hinblick auf die Prinzipien der Verfassung und der Unabhängigkeitserklärung. In Anbetracht der kulturellen, regionalen, rassischen und ethnischen Unterschiede des Landes ist dieser Konsens um so bemerkenswerter.

A more vehement and widespread upheaval resulted from the objection of a large segment of the population to the Vietnam War. This caused an angry protest movement (e.g. draft resistors, protest marches) and saw the inability of two successive administrations (Johnson, Nixon) to quell it. The war engendered deep distrust of government, especially among draft age students, and particularly in the Executive Branch. Nixon's highhanded methods, especially his handling of the war and of dissenters, led to the most acute political crisis since the Civil War: the Watergate affair and the resignation of President Nixon in 1974, a first in American history. The nature of Nixon's intentions continues to be hotly debated. The strength of the political system (e.g., the press, Congressional leadership, judicial stability, individual courage) ultimately prevailed.

The Vietnam War and Watergate also exposed the shift of power from the Legislature to the Executive that had been progressively taking place (the "imperial presidency"). In reaction, reformers attempted to introduce what they considered to be more democratic methods of nominating candidates for political office. Notable are primaries which proliferated in the late 1960's. The power pendulum also swung toward Congress during the Ford and Carter administrations. Among the reforms introduced were the War Powers Act; the Privacy Act and the amendments to the Freedom of Information Act; establishment of a Congressional budget office; and self-disciplining efforts such as the Congressional Ethics Committees.

The rise of single-interest pressure groups, especially in the 1970's, has occasionally threatened to stymie the progress of important legislation. Among the most important of these pressure groups have been large corporations and the military; indeed, President Eisenhower warned about the "military-industrial complex" in 1961. In part because of this difficulty, Americans have increasingly turned toward the Judiciary for resolution of previously non-judicial concerns. Many of these issues reached the Supreme Court, which under the leadership of Earl Warren (1953–1969) handed down important decisions extending the rights of minorities, protecting the rights of accused persons, and intervening to bring about the reapportionment of state legislatures and the national House of Representatives.

Throughout these crises, the political system has been flexible. This stability stems from a broad consensus behind the principles embodied in the Constitution and the Declaration of Independence. This consensus is all the more remarkable given the cultural, regional, racial, and ethnic diversity of the country.

II. Die Vereinigten Staaten als Weltmacht

a) Die Situation am Ende des Zweiten Weltkrieges und der Beginn des Kalten Krieges

Eines der vordringlichsten Ziele der Vereinigten Staaten während des Zweiten Weltkrieges war die Errichtung eines dauerhaften Friedens unter Einschluß einer Wirtschaftsordnung, die auf einer Politik des Freihandels und stabiler Währungen beruhte. Im Gegensatz zur Rolle, die die Vereinigten Staaten am Ende des Ersten Weltkrieges spielten, übernahm das Land bei der Lösung der kriegsbedingten Probleme nun die Führung. Die Vereinigten Staaten spielten eine Schlüsselrolle bei der Gründung der Vereinten Nationen und vermieden den Rückzug in den Isolationismus, der ihre Außenpolitik nach dem Ersten Weltkrieg charakterisiert hatte. Sie halfen vielen der vom Krieg zerstörten Länder und förderten, wo das möglich war, die Errichtung liberaler Demokratien. Gleichwohl scheiterten Versuche, im chinesischen Bürgerkrieg zu vermitteln und das nationalchinesische Regime zu unterstützen.

Das Bündnis, das Hitler-Deutschland besiegt hatte, brach in den späten 40er Jahren auseinander. Der daraus sich entwickelnde „Kalte Krieg" war besonders zwischen 1947 und 1955 durch eine Verschärfung der Beziehungen zwischen der Sowjetunion und ihren Alliierten auf der einen und den Vereinigten Staaten und ihren westlichen Verbündeten auf der anderen Seite gekennzeichnet. Die Gründe für das Entstehen des Kalten Krieges sind nach wie vor Gegenstand wissenschaftlicher Kontroverse. Indem sie die Sowjetunion beschuldigen, während des Krieges getroffene Übereinkünfte verletzt und osteuropäische Staaten unterjocht zu haben, machen einige Autoren die Sowjetunion für den „Kalten Krieg" verantwortlich. Andere betonen, daß die Sowjetunion ihre Einflußsphäre in Osteuropa behaupten mußte. Wieder andere schließlich machen beide Seiten verantwortlich.

Im Zuge des Ost-West-Konflikts entstand ein weitgespanntes Netz von Bündnissen. Das wichtigste westliche Bündnis ist die 1949 gegründete NATO. Dieses Bündnis und andere wie SEATO (1954), CENTO (1959), ANZUS (1951) sowie der Verteidigungsvertrag mit Japan (1951) markierten einen entscheidenden Bruch mit der traditionellen amerikanischen Politik, die in Friedenszeiten bestrebt gewesen war, sich nicht in „verwirrende Bündnisse" zu verstricken.

b) Der Wiederaufbau Europas nach dem II. Weltkrieg

In den Vereinigten Staaten setzte sich die Erkenntnis durch, daß ohne wirtschaftlichen Wiederaufbau wenig Aussicht auf Stabilität in den vom Krieg zerstörten Ländern Europas bestand. Der Marshall-Plan von 1947 sorgte für ein umfangreiches wirtschaftliches Stützungsprogramm für Westeuropa, um damit den Europäern wieder eine menschenwürdige Existenz zu ermöglichen. Er förderte den Freihandel zwischen den europäischen Staaten sowie zwischen diesen und den Vereinigten Staaten, und er trug möglicherweise dazu bei, die politische Attraktivität des Rechts- wie des Linksradikalismus zu schwächen. Er förderte europäische Einigungsbestrebungen, die schließlich in der Europäischen Gemeinschaft verwirklicht wurden.

c) Die Vereinigten Staaten und die Dritte Welt

Beim Bestreben, die weniger entwickelten Länder wirtschaftlich zu unterstützen (Trumans Punkt 4 von 1949) nahmen die Vereinigten Staaten in der Nachkriegszeit eine führende Rolle ein. In mancher Hinsicht versuchten sie, den Erfolg der Marshall-Plan-Hilfe zu wiederholen: Sie waren bestrebt, die Volkswirtschaften der Entwicklungsländer zu kräftigen, indem sie neue Handelsbeziehungen knüpften und politische Bedingungen schufen, die diese Länder gegen das Wirken von Kräften immun machen sollten, die von den Vereinigten

II. The U.S. as a World Power

a) The Situation at the End of World War II and the Beginning of the Cold War

One of the foremost aims of the United States during World War II was the establishment of a lasting peace including the formulation of an economic order based upon open trade relations and stable monetary policies. Contrary to the role played by the U.S. at the end of World War I, the country took the lead in resolving problems resulting from the war; it played a key role in the founding of the United Nations and avoided the retreat into isolationism which had characterized its foreign policy after World War I. It assisted many countries ravaged by the war and wherever possible supported the establishment of liberal democracies. However, attempts to mediate in the Chinese Civil War and to prop up the Nationalist regime in China failed.

The alliance that defeated Hitler Germany broke up in the late 1940's. The resulting "cold war" featured a hardening, especially between 1947 and 1955, of relations between the Soviet Union and its allies and the United States and its allies in the West. The reasons for the Cold War remain a subject of controversy. Some interpretors blame the Soviet Union, arguing that it broke wartime agreements and subjugated East European states; other writers emphasize the need of the Soviet Union to maintain its own sphere of influence in Eastern Europe; still other scholars accuse both sides.

The resultant East-West conflict led the U.S. to establish wide-ranging alliances, the most important of which in the West was NATO (1949). This alliance, and others such as SEATO (1954), CENTO (1959), ANZUS (1951), and the defense treaty with Japan (1951) were a major departure from traditional U.S. policy which had sought to avoid "entangling" alliances in peacetime.

b) European Recovery

The U.S. recognized that without economic recovery there was little prospect for stability in the war-torn countries of Europe. The European Recovery Program ("Marshall Plan") of 1947 provided massive economic assistance to Western Europe, in order that their people might regain their human dignity. It also established a policy of freer trade among the European states and between them and the United States and may have lessened the political appeal of political forces of both the extreme Right and the extreme Left. It promoted European unification efforts which eventually led to the European Community.

c) The U.S. and the Third World

The U.S. became the leader in the post-war years in supplying economic assistance to the less developed countries (Truman's Point 4 – 1949). In many ways, the U.S. sought to duplicate the results of the European Recovery Program: to strengthen the economies of the developing countries, thereby stimulating new trade opportunities and creating political situations which would insulate these countries against what the U.S. perceived as subversive

Staaten als subversiv empfunden wurden. Als entsprechende Versuche in einer Reihe von Ländern fehlschlugen, sahen sich die Vereinigten Staaten gezwungen, etablierte Regime, selbst wenn es sich um Diktaturen handelte, als Partner zu akzeptieren, ohne auf politischem Wandel zu bestehen. Während die Vereinigten Staaten ihre umfangreiche Entwicklungshilfe fortsetzten, sahen sie sich als Führungsmacht der westlichen Welt mit einer wachsenden Opposition durch die Länder der Dritten Welt konfrontiert, die im Ost-West-Konflikt ihre Neutralität zu wahren bestrebt waren und einen schnellen Weg aus dem Jahrhunderte währenden Zustand kolonialer Abhängigkeit und wirtschaftlicher Ausbeutung suchten. Als Versuche der Vereinigten Staaten, einen für möglich gehaltenen Umsturz der extremen Linken in einigen Ländern (z.B. Iran 1953, Guatemala 1954, Kuba 1961, Chile 1973) zu verhindern, an die Öffentlichkeit drangen, erhielt diese Opposition Auftrieb. Auf der anderen Seite waren die Vereinigten Staaten bemüht, dem Frieden in der Welt als Vermittler zu dienen, besonders im arabisch-israelischen Konflikt. Seit den späten 70er Jahren vermieden die Vereinigten Staaten in wachsendem Maße Eingriffe in die inneren Angelegenheiten anderer Länder. Sie setzten jedoch ihr Entwicklungshilfeprogramm, sowohl zweiseitig (AID) als auch durch internationale Organisationen (Weltbank, OECD, UNIDO, usw.) vermittelt, fort.

d) Der Vietnam-Krieg

Zwischen der Mitte der 50er Jahre, als die Regierung Eisenhower Südvietnam zu stabilisieren versuchte, und 1975, als der letzte Amerikaner Vietnam verließ, verstrickten sich die Vereinigten Staaten in ständig wachsendem Ausmaß in die Probleme dieser Region. Dieses Engagement hatte eine Reihe von Ursachen: die traditionelle Feindseligkeit der Amerikaner gegenüber dem Kommunismus; die Überzeugung, daß die Volksrepublik China den Kommunismus in ganz Asien schüre und bei diesem Unterfangen eingedämmt werden müsse; den Wunsch politischer Führer in Amerika, besonders von Präsident Lyndon Johnson, die gegenüber Alliierten eingegangenen Verpflichtungen zu erfüllen und die amerikanische Glaubwürdigkeit („credibility") aufrechtzuerhalten; die Überzeugung amerikanischer Experten, daß es auch für komplexe soziale und kulturelle Probleme militärische und technologische Lösungen gäbe, sowie die von Spitzenpolitikern gehegte Überzeugung, daß der Krieg in Vietnam in erster Linie eine Auseinandersetzung zwischen kommunistischen und nichtkommunistischen Kräften sei. Viele Amerikaner, die diese Sicht der Dinge zurückwiesen, vertraten die Ansicht, daß der Krieg in erster Linie ein Bürgerkrieg sei; andere unterstellten den Vereinigten Staaten neokolonialistische Bestrebungen.

Die in den frühen 60er Jahren einsetzende Teilnahme amerikanischer Soldaten im Krieg führte jedoch nicht dazu, daß Amerika seine Ziele erreichte. An der Erfolglosigkeit des amerikanischen Einsatzes änderte sich auch nichts nach der Massierung amerikanischer Truppen – auf der Höhe des Engagements 1968 belief sich ihre Zahl auf mehr als 500000 – und nach den schweren Bombenangriffen, die Nord- wie Südvietnam verwüsteten. Als Mitte der 60er Jahre der Krieg eskalierte, vermehrten sich die Proteste in den Vereinigten Staaten. Angesichts der inneren Unruhe nahm Präsident Richard Nixon, der seit 1969 im Amt war, Zuflucht zu einer Reihe von Maßnahmen, einschließlich des geheimen Bombardements von Laos und Kambodscha und einer Invasion Kambodschas. Selbst durch diese Anstrengungen gelang es nicht, eine militärische Wende herbeizuführen, so daß die Regierung Nixon Anfang 1973 einem etappenweisen Rückzug zustimmte. Der Rückzug der amerikanischen Truppen besiegelte das Schicksal der Regierung von Südvietnam, die 1975 fiel. In der Nachkriegszeit war das Verhältnis der Vereinigten Staaten zu Vietnam unter anderem durch folgendes gekennzeichnet: die Nichtanerkennung Vietnams durch die Vereinigten Staaten, die zum Teil ihre Ursache darin hatte, daß der Verbleib vermißter amerikanischer Soldaten nicht

elements. When this failed in a number of countries, the U.S. felt compelled to accept established regimes, even dictatorships, as partners without insisting on political changes. While continuing to provide a large amount of development assistance, the U.S., as leader of the West, found itself increasingly opposed by the newly-independent Third World nations who wished to remain neutral in the East-West conflict and who sought a quick redress for centuries of colonial status and economic exploitation. When it became clear that the U.S. had intervened to prevent a perceived swing to the far Left in several countries (e.g., Iran, 1953; Guatemala, 1954; Cuba, 1961; Chile, 1973), this criticism gained strength. On the other hand, the U.S. tried to serve world peace as a mediator, particularly in the Arab-Israeli conflict. In the late 1970's, the U.S. increasingly tried to avoid intervention abroad but continued its economic assistance program both bilaterally (AID) and through international agencies (World Bank, OECD, UNIDO, etc.).

d) The Vietnam War

Between the mid-1950's, when the administration of President Dwight D. Eisenhower propped up South Vietnam, and 1975, when the last American left Vietnam, the United States became increasingly involved in the region. Many forces impelled this commitment: the traditional hostility of Americans to communism; the conviction that the People's Republic of China was fomenting communism throughout Asia and needed to be contained; the desire of America's political leaders, especially President Lyndon Johnson, to fulfill obligations to Allies and to sustain American credibility; the faith of American experts in military and technological solutions to complex social and cultural problems; and the belief of top officials that the struggle in Vietnam was primarily between Communist and non-Communist forces. Many Americans who rejected this view argued that the struggle was primarily a civil war; others identified the United States with neo-Colonialism.

The participation of American soldiers in the war, which began in the early 1960's, did not succeed in achieving American objectives. This lack of success persisted even after the enormous commitment of American soldiers – more than 500,000 at the peak of involvement in 1968 – and of heavy bombing raids that devastated both South and North Vietnam. As the war escalated in the mid-1960's, domestic protests mounted in the United States. Faced with such unrest, President Richard Nixon, who took office in 1969, tried a variety of expedients, including secret bombings of Laos and Cambodia and an invasion of Cambodia. But these efforts, too, failed to turn the tide of battle, and in early 1973 the Nixon administration finally agreed to a phased withdrawal. This withdrawal of American troops ensured the doom of the South Vietnamese government, which fell by 1975. In the postwar period, the U.S. relationship with Vietnam was characterized, among other things, by non-recognition, attributed by some to the failure to account for missing American

aufgeklärt wurde; das Ausbleiben amerikanischer Hilfe für den Wiederaufbau; den großen vietnamesischen Flüchtlingsstrom in die Vereinigten Staaten.

Der lange Krieg und seine Auswirkungen scheinen bewirkt zu haben, daß Amerika seinen politischen und militärischen Verbindlichkeiten realistischere Grenzen setzte. Zu den mittelbaren Folgen des Vietnam-Krieges gehört, daß die Bürger gegenüber den Gefahren eines Mißbrauchs der exekutiven Gewalt wachsamer geworden sind. Gleichwohl scheint der Krieg innerhalb weniger Jahre in weite Ferne gerückt; anscheinend wünschten die Amerikaner, ihn zu vergessen. Deshalb ist es auch unklar, ob der Krieg nennenswerten Wandel in Amerikas Außen- und Militärpolitik verursacht hat; unmittelbar führte er zum Ende der allgemeinen Wehrpflicht.

e) Koexistenz und Entspannung

Während der härtesten Phase des Kalten Krieges (1947–1955) waren die Spannungen zwischen Ost und West durch ein sich schnell verschärfendes Wettrüsten, durch die Entwicklung der Wasserstoffbombe und durch die anhaltende Verwicklung der Vereinigten Staaten in Ostasien – einschließlich des Korea-Krieges (1950–1953) – bestimmt. Beginnend mit der Genfer Konferenz von 1955, durch die Kuba-Krise (1962) intensiviert, begannen die Vereinigten Staaten und die Sowjetunion, nach Wegen zu suchen, um die Spannungen zu mildern (Politik der „Koexistenz"). Weitere Schritte in dieser Richtung waren Atomwaffenteststoppverträge, Verträge über die Nichtverbreitung von Kernwaffen, SALT. Ohne daß grundlegende Gegensätze ausgeräumt werden konnten, führten diese Bemühungen jedoch auf einigen Gebieten zu begrenzter Kooperation („Détente"). Zeitweilig beobachteten Amerikas europäische Verbündete direkte amerikanisch-sowjetische Verhandlungen mit Sorge, weil sie die Möglichkeit eines Ausgleichs auf ihre Kosten befürchteten. Solche Befürchtungen führten zu vermehrten Konsultationen innerhalb der NATO mit dem Ziel, die Positionen im westlichen Bündnis soweit wie möglich aufeinander abzustimmen. Forcierte sowjetische Rüstungsanstrengungen auf solchen Gebieten, auf denen die Sowjetunion nicht durch Verträge gebunden war, die sowjetische Invasion in Afghanistan und andere sowjetische Aktivitäten trugen dazu bei, daß innerhalb der amerikanischen Führungsspitze am Ende der achten Dekade der Nutzen der Entspannungspolitik zunehmend in Zweifel gezogen wurde.

servicemen; by a failure of the U.S. to provide reconstruction assistance; and by the large influx of Vietnamese refugees into the U.S.

In the aftermath of the war, it appeared that the prolonged conflict forced America to set more realistic limits to its political and military commitments, and that it alerted the citizenry to the potential dangers in the use of executive powers. Within a few years, however, the war seemed remote; Americans appeared to wish to forget it. It is, therefore, unclear whether the war caused major changes in America's foreign and military policies; it did lead to the immediate end of the draft.

e) Coexistence and Détente

During the harshest phase of the Cold War (1947–1955), tensions between the East and West included a rapidly escalating arms race, the development of the hydrogen bomb and the continuing involvement of the United States in East Asia, including the Korean War (1950–1953). Beginning in 1955 (Geneva Conference) and intensified after the Cuban Missile Crisis (1962), the U.S. and the Soviet Union began to seek ways to defuse these tensions ("coexistence"). Later steps toward this end included test-ban treaties, non-proliferation treaties, SALT. They led to limited cooperation in certain areas without removing basic antagonisms ("détente"). America's European allies were at times concerned about direct U.S.-Soviet negotiations because they feared the possibility of an agreement at their expense; these concerns strengthened the consultative processes of NATO to create a united Western position whenever possible. An intensified Soviet arms program concentrating on those areas not covered by arms agreements, the Soviet invasion of Afghanistan, and Soviet activities elsewhere were among the factors which caused American political leaders to question the value of détente at the end of the eighth decade.

III. Die Vereinigten Staaten und Deutschland

a) Besatzungspolitik

Die amerikanische Besatzungspolitik war in demjenigen Teil Deutschlands, der sich unter ihrer Verwaltung befand, durch energische Entnazifizierung, Entmilitarisierung und die gleichzeitig vorgenommene „re-orientation" der übrigen Bevölkerung gekennzeichnet. Die Konzepte einer „Kollektivschuld" und der „Entindustrialisierung" (Morgenthauplan) wurden niemals offizielle amerikanische Politik. Es wurde versucht, demokratische Institutionen zu errichten. Dabei griff man auf Konzepte zurück, deren Nutzen frühere Perioden der deutschen Geschichte – besonders die Weimarer Zeit – belegt hatten. Werthaltungen und Institutionen, deren relative Schwäche während der Weimarer Republik zum Aufstieg des NS-Regimes beigetragen hatte, wurden gestärkt. Wirtschaftliche Stabilität konnte erst erreicht werden, als die Produktionsbeschränkungen für die Industrien aufgehoben wurden, die Kredithilfe des Marshallplans verstärkt wurde und die Währungsreform (1948) durchgeführt worden war. Die amerikanische Besatzungsmacht stellte die Frage der Verstaatlichung der Industrien zurück und überwies die Entscheidung an die künftige Bundesrepublik. Noch vor dem Inkrafttreten des Besatzungsstatus und der förmlichen Gründung der Bundesrepublik (1949) wurde sukzessive deutschen Institutionen – lokalen und regionalen Behörden, Gerichten, Banken, Gewerkschaften, Zeitungen, Rundfunkstationen usw. – eigene Verantwortung übertragen.

b) Die Teilung Deutschlands und das Berlinproblem

Da die Siegermächte des Zweiten Weltkriegs sich nicht auf einen Friedensvertrag für Deutschland als Ganzes einigen konnten, entschieden sich die Westmächte, auf ihrem Besatzungsterritorium die Gründung der Bundesrepublik Deutschland zu authorisieren. Die Sowjetunion gründete die DDR (1949). Die Westmächte waren entschlossen, ihre Verantwortung für Berlin aufrechtzuerhalten. Als die Sowjetunion die Stadt 1948 einer Blockade unterwarf, errichteten die Vereinigten Staaten eine Luftbrücke, um die Versorgung sicherzustellen. Die Verteidigung der Stadt und das Wohlergehen ihrer Einwohner ist nach wie vor ein zentrales Anliegen der Vereinigten Staaten. Sie wahren ihre im Vier-Mächte-Abkommen von 1971 definierten Rechte.

c) Die Vereinigten Staaten und die Bundesrepublik Deutschland

Der Gründung der Bundesrepublik Deutschland lief die Erweiterung ihrer Sicherheitsgarantie durch die Vereinigten Staaten sowie ihre sukzessive vollzogene Einbeziehung in das westliche militärische und politische Sicherheitssystem (NATO, WEU) parallel. In dem Maße, in dem die Bundesrepublik wirtschaftliche Stärke und politische Unabhängigkeit erlangte, entwickelte sich die Beziehung zu den Vereinigten Staaten auf zahlreichen Gebieten zu einem Verhältnis wechselseitiger Abhängigkeit, wobei die Vereinigten Staaten als Weltmacht und die Bundesrepublik als eine der führenden europäischen Mächte agierten. Die deutsche Ostpolitik war mit den Vereinigten Staaten und anderen westlichen Alliierten abgesprochen.

Die enge Partnerschaft sowie die Interessen- und Werteübereinstimmung auf vielen Gebieten haben dazu geführt, daß die Bundesrepublik einer der zuverlässigsten Verbündeten der Vereinigten Staaten wurde. Als in den späten 70er Jahren neue Probleme von internationalem Ausmaß entstanden (Energiekrise, neue militärische Bedrohungen, Probleme der Geldwertstabilität), erwiesen sich die in früheren Jahren eingespielten Mechanismen gegenseitiger Konsultationen als nützliches Mittel, um Differenzen auszuräumen.

III. The U.S. and Germany

a) Occupation Policies

U.S. occupation policies in the part of Germany under its jurisdiction were characterized by an effort at quick denazification, demilitarization and a simultaneous reorientation of the remainder of the population. The concepts of "Kollektivschuld" and "de-industrialization" (the Morgenthau Plan) never became official U.S. policy. Attempts were made to establish democratic institutions, using concepts whose value had been demonstrated during previous periods of German history, particularly the Weimar period, and by strengthening values and institutions whose relative weakness during the Weimar period had contributed to the rise of the National Socialist regime. The economic stability of the country could not be reestablished until there was a lessening of the limits set on industrial production, the extension of credit through the Marshall Plan and currency reform (1948). American occupation authorities deferred the question of the nationalization of industry pending decision by a future German Federal Republic. There was a steady devolution of responsiblity to German institutions – local and regional governments, courts, banks, trade unions, newspapers, radio stations, etc. – even prior to the enactment of the Occupation Statute and the establishment of the Federal Republic (1949).

b) The Division of Germany and the Problem of Berlin

Following the failure of the victorious powers to agree on terms of a peace treaty for all of Germany, the Western powers decided to authorize the establishment of the Federal Republic in their zones of occupation, and the Soviet Union established the German Democratic Republic (1949). The Western powers decided to maintain their responsibilities in Berlin. When the Soviet Union blockaded the city in 1948, the U.S. mounted an airlift to sustain it. The U.S. continues to be committed to its defense and to the well-being of its people, and maintains its rights as defined in the Four-Power Agreement of 1971.

c) The U.S. and the Federal Republic

The establishment of the Federal Republic proceeded simultaneously with the extension of security guarantees to it and its eventual inclusion in the Western military and political security system (NATO, WEU). As the Federal Republic grew in economic strength and political independence, the relationship with the United States increasingly became one of interdependence in many fields, with the U.S. pursuing its goals as a world power, and the Federal Republic acting as a major regional power in Europe. German détente policies ("Ostpolitik") were coordinated with the U.S. and other Western Allies.

The close partnership and large-scale congruity of interests and values has led the Federal Republic to become one of America's strongest allies. As new international problems arose in the late 1970's (energy, new military threats, currency stabilization), the consultative processes established in the earlier period proved a valuable tool in overcoming differences.

Obgleich Amerikaner und Deutsche sich in zwei Weltkriegen als Feinde gegenüberstanden, sind sie durch Überzeugungen und Vorstellungen miteinander eng verbunden, die von beiden Seiten geteilt werden. Die wirtschaftlichen und politischen Abhängigkeiten zwischen beiden Ländern beruhen offenbar nicht nur auf gemeinsamen Interessen, sondern ebenso auf gemeinsamen Werthaltungen und einander ähnlichen Lebensweisen. Dieser Konsens wird nicht notwendigerweise von allen Individuen, Gruppen und Klassen geteilt, da in beiden Ländern pluralistische Gesellschaften bestehen und Werthaltungen und Wünsche, abhängig von Klassenzugehörigkeit, Alter, Religion, Geschlecht, regionaler Zugehörigkeit und – besonders in den Vereinigten Staaten – rassischen und ethnischen Gruppierungen, erheblich differieren. Gelegentlich sind engere Beziehungen zwischen vergleichbaren Gruppen beider Gesellschaften als zwischen den verschiedenen Gruppen innerhalb einer Gesellschaft zu beobachten. In der Arbeiterschaft und in der Mittelschicht beider Länder existieren, was Arbeitsethik, den Glauben an den Nutzen materiellen Fortschritts und das Verlangen nach Effizienz und Innovation betrifft, ähnliche Werte und Wünsche. Teile der Jugend in beiden Ländern werden zur Überwindung dessen, was sie an der Sozialstruktur und an traditionellen Konventionen als veraltet empfinden, von vergleichbaren Impulsen angetrieben.

Im Ganzen gesehen wird deutlich, daß in der Geschichte beider Länder die Beziehungen kaum jemals enger als in der Nachkriegszeit gewesen sind. Interessenübereinstimmung und Wertekonsens haben, neben anderem, intensiven kulturellen Austausch bewirkt. Von gelegentlich auftauchender Kritik sowie zeitweilig zu beobachtendem Ausbruch antiamerikanischer oder antideutscher Emotionen abgesehen, sind die deutsch-amerikanischen Beziehungen durch gegenseitigen Respekt und wechselseitiges Vertrauen gekennzeichnet.

Though Americans and Germans fought as enemies in two world wars, many commonly held attitudes and mutual perceptions connect the societies of the two countries. The close economic and political interdependence obviously is based not solely on common interests, but also on common values and life styles. This consensus is not necessarily shared by all individuals, groups, and classes, for pluralism exists in both countries and there are considerable differences in values and aspirations within each society depending on class, age, religion, sex, regional orientation, and, especially in the United States, race and ethnic grouping. At times, there are closer ties between similar groups in the two countries than between the various groups in either of them. In the middle and working classes of both nations there are comparable values and aspirations, e.g., work ethic, belief in the advantages of material progress, and the quest for efficiency and innovation. Segments of the youth of both countries have similar interests in overcoming what they perceive to be outmoded portions of the traditional social structure and traditional conventions.

On the whole it is clear that in the history of the two countries the bilateral relationship has hardly ever been closer than in the postwar period. A congruence of interests and a consensus of values have, among other manifestations, led to an extensive cultural interchange. Occasional criticism and the expression of anti-American or anti-German emotions notwithstanding, the German-American relationship is marked by mutual respect and trust.

Gerald R. Kleinfeld

The Federal Republic of Germany in American College and University Textbooks for Courses in Western Civilization

Most United States colleges and universities, including community or junior colleges, teach a basic introductory course in western civilization. Traditionally, this has been a required course in the general education curriculum but, as requirements changed, it has occasionally been removed from the required list. Recent developments see some return to the list for the western civilization course. Students majoring in any discipline may elect the western civilization course, and many choose it to fulfill required or recommended course lists. Thus, while it does not have the share of enrollment it once enjoyed as a course almost universally required, it still reaches an extremely broad cross-section of students. It is also often the first, and only, reference that most college students will have to the history of the Federal Republic of Germany. This ist especially true since the number of students selecting a major field in Germany language and literature continues to decline.

The plan of instruction and structure of western civilization courses is not uniform across the nation and, although the customary duration is two semesters, some courses begin at an earlier point in history than others. Thus, because all extend to the present time, some are more highly compressed than others. Except for the problem of which point at which to break the two semesters, the time frame is not generally reflected in textbooks. Individual instructors pass more rapidly over some periods than others. In an analysis of the treatment of the Federal Republic of Germany in western civilization textbooks, therefore, the time frame involved plays a generally minor role in differentiation. Much more fundamental is the question of structure and approach. Textbooks are selected by professors on an individual basis, and there are no statewide selections for universities or colleges. In some departments of history, the professors teaching the western civilization course meet and vote on a single text to be used in their classes. This is rare and, even then, the individual professors will require or recommend supplemental books on a variety of subjects, or even anthologies and special purpose books, while structuring their lectures and class assignments according to their own approach to the course. Some professors require a considerable number of supplemental books. Some purposely structure their lectures to offer different perspectives than those in the basic textbook. Generally, however, the standard western civilization textbook is a basic study and reference volume for the student and considerably aids in structuring his/her approach to the general framework of the history of western man excluding the United States.

Publishers of textbooks have always sought to find the broadest applicability for their products. Where one text could not serve, some publishers have offered two, or three, or more. An analysis of the currently available textbooks indicates that they may be divided into certain categories according to structure and approach. Such categories might be:

A. older textbooks which have been revised expanded and updated to the present time

B. newer textbooks which retain traditional structure and approach

C. newer textbooks with modified or completely new structure and approach

Typically, the textbooks of Category A have largely ended their treatment of western civilization in reaching the conclusion of World War II. They tend to have one or more chapters on the "postwar" period in Europe without considering the recent past in and for itself. This may partly reflect the reluctance of some historians to teach the contemporary world. The Federal Republic of Germany, therefore, is seen in such textbooks of Category A largely in "postwar" terms.

Category B textbooks have been written from a standpoint of the continuity of history to the present. They have abandoned the "postwar" approach and tend to treat the recent past with the same type of broader coverage assigned to earlier periods. This permits not only greater detail, but also deeper analysis.

The textbooks of Category C apply international and cross-cultural analysis to the contemporary world, and some of them do the same to the entire course of European history. Therefore, while it is relatively easy to identify sections on the Federal Republic of Germany in books of A and B, even though the approach may be different, there are few such sections in the books of C. In fact the non-national perspective results in a dispersal of the treatment of the Federal Republic within several chapters and sections. Any quantitative and qualitative analysis must take this dispersal into account.

The following is a brief analysis of the treatment of the history of the Federal Republic of Germany in ten of the most widely used western civilization textbooks. The subject references are the most frequent topics applied to the Federal Republic of Germany by the authors of those textbooks, and are not intended to be a uniform list of desirable themes.

CATEGORY A

Brinton, Crane; Christopher, John B.; Wolff, Robert Lee. *A History of Civilization.* 5th ed. Englewood Cliffs, New Jersey: Prentice-Hall, Inc., 1976.

International Affairs: The role of Germany as a worn-torn bone of contention between the Soviet Union and the United States is used as a device to describe the partition of Germany and the Berlin troubles. The discussion leads up to a more detailed description of the history of the Federal Republic.

Government and Society: West German political developments are traced from the formation of the republic to the fall of Brandt. The German rapid economic revival is described, but there is little in the way of analysis as to why recovery was so spectacular. Political and constitutional developments are treated in general terms, and few personalities are given detailed coverage. The West German Basic Law is discussed and contrasted with the Weimar Constitution. Lack of support for either left or right wing extremist groups is emphasized. Strict adherence of the West German government to constitutional and democratic principles is also stressed. Compared to Brandt, relatively little space is devoted to the personality and policies of Adenauer. *Ostpolitik* is described, but the book maintains that Brandt's disdain for domestic politics and the problems of labor brought him into conflict with the left wing of his own party. In moments of crisis, Brandt seemed to become oddly indecisive. Schmidt is characterized as lacking the flair and personal appeal of Brandt; his great strength rests in his administrative talents and his ability to handle economic problems. The Common Market is described and discussed. In general, this text treats the Federal Republic alongside other West European countries in comparative paragraphs outlining the salient features of domestic history and foreign policy. The reader has no real appreciation of the dynamics of German history since 1945.

Palmer, R. R., and Colton, Joel. *A History of the Modern World.* 5th ed. New York: Alfred A. Knopf, 1978.

In addition to some isolated references in the section on the Cold War, the Federal Republic of Germany is discussed in a compact unit covering the period from 1945 to the resignation of Brandt. According to the authors, the Basic Law was designed to prevent a repetition of the problems encountered with the Weimar Constitution. Adenauer, they write, had a personality and political style which could be compared to Bismarck's, but during his chancellorship West Germany developed stable democratic government and an aversion to extreme political positions. In context, Brandt's political style is characterized as more flamboyant and ready to take risks. *Ostpolitik* is partially an extension of this. Thus, Brandt breaks with Adenauer's inflexible foreign policy and opens a dialogue with the East. The West German economy in the 1970s is compared favorably to the American economy in the same period. West Germany's steady prosperity is the envy and admiration of both friend and foe. A final paragraph describes how the desire for reunification of the immediate post-war years has begun to wane as the people of East and West Germany become more accustomed to the division. Citizens of the two states have begun to view each other as "foreigners", and many are recalling that Germany was only united for the brief period from 1871–1945.

This text offers the student a coherent description of the history and development of the Federal Republic with an attempt to explain basic issues and problems both of foreign and domestic policy. Although compact and brief, it does leave the reader with an impression of politics and economics, and even social and other questions.

Strayer, Joseph R., and Gatzke, Hans W. *The Mainstream of Civilization.* 3rd ed. New York: Harcourt Brace Jovanovich, Inc., 1979.

International Affairs: Stress is laid on Soviet fears of a strong Germany as a major factor in the East-West dispute over German future that led to partition. The book presents a traditional narrative of the events leading to the establishment of the Federal Republic and the critical period of the Berlin airlift. This is followed by a discussion of the origins of NATO and the Common Market.

Government and Society: Just as the discussion of the postwar period emphasized Soviet and French fears based on past experiences, the political analysis considered German fears of a revival of old domestic troubles. In this connection, reunification and rearmament were the biggest issues facing West Germany. Reunification might unleash a militant nationalism that would also seek to restore territories lost to Poland after World War II. Most Germans, the authors point out, came to accept division. They "might never live to see their country united". The authors argue that the war discredited all right wing extremism, and that Adenauer's pro-Western foreign policies created excellent relations with France and the United States at the expense of the Soviet Union and eastern Europe, threatening possible reunification with East Germany. Brandt's *Ostpolitik* redressed the balance by calming Soviet bloc fears of German strength while maintaining strong ties with the West. Meanwhile, the "middle of the road" Christian Democrats have gradually given way to the "moderately leftist" Social Democrats as Brandt succeeded Kiesinger. Later, Brandt resigns "over a domestic issue", and Schmidt is described as "equally able". The authors state that the West German economy is based upon a "traditional policy of laissez faire", and contrast this with the nationalization policies pursued in the United Kingdom. The strength of the West German economy compared to their own led many other west European states which had engaged in nationalization programs to envy the strong free-market economy of the German Federal Republic.

Other Points: The authors discuss the spread of left-wing terrorism throughout western Europe in the 70s. In West Germany, they report, government crackdowns on terrorism excited fears of growing authoritarianism and repression. The authors dismiss those fears as groundless. The section on the Federal Republic is very brief, the same length as those on France and Italy, for example, and gives little opportunity for the student to understand domestic developments.

Burns, Edward McNall; Lerner, Robert E.; Meacham, Standish. *Western Civilizations: Their History and Their Culture.* 9th ed. New York: W. W. Norton and Company, 1980.

This is the latest of a long series of revisions of an older textbook. Post World War II history is added on in a world-history frame work. West Germany is only mentioned in this book as the source of many problems straining East-West relations. There is no discussion of Adenauer, Brandt, or any other figure or issue in West German politics. Discussion moves along from one Cold War crisis to another. After 1945, this book becomes supranational in scope and is concerned only with broad worldwide trends and movements. West Germany is never discussed as a separate political and social entity. The country's economic revival is only considered in connection with the Marshall Plan and other American efforts to rebuild war-torn western Europe.

Burns, Edward McNall and Talph, Philip Lee. *World Civilizations.* 5th ed. New York: W. W. Norton and Company, 1974.

A re-formation of the Western Civilization book analyzed above, this textbook is a history of the entire world, thus it is short on space and concentrates on broad trends and movements. Germany after World War II is mentioned mainly as a source of tension between East and West. Soviet fears of a militarily and industrially revived Germany clash with American desires for a strong first line of defense against threatening communism. This book is distinguishable more for what it lacks than for what it has. As an example, there is some discussion of German economic recovery in conjunction with American assistance programs, but no mention of Adenauer, Brandt, or any other name or event in West German politics. Nor is there any discussion of society and culture in the Federal Republic.

Wallbank, T. Walter; Taylor, Alastair M.; Bailkey, Nels M. *Civilization: Past and Present.* 7th ed. Glenview, Illinois: Scott Foresman and Company, 1976.

This is a widely used book which has a series of chapters on post-World War II Europe and the rest of the world. The East-West conflict is a major topic. Following these chapters is another series on new states in Africa and Asia, new life styles, and major issues of current world events. Germany and other European countries receive little mention. There is some reference to West German economic recovery, stressing American aid, and of the German desire for reunification, itself a result of the Cold War-created division of the country. Brandt is mentioned because of his *Ostpolitik,* described as a symbol of East-West détente. Schmidt had succeeded Brandt when the book went to press, and was not expected to pursue *Ostpolitik* with the same enthusiasm as Brandt. Beyond these brief references, there is little discussion of the Federal Republic of Germany.

CATEGORY B

Kagan, Donald; Ozment, Steven; Turner, Frank M. *The Western Heritage.* New York: Macmillan Publishing Company, Inc., 1979.

A traditional, though new, textbook, *The Western Heritage* has a large section on post-World War II Europe in which the Cold War is a major subject. The early years of the Federal Republic of Germany, the Berlin Crises, and NATO are described here. A later section on European international developments treats the origins and success of the European Community.

Government & Society: A separate heading, among several dealing with specific states, is entitled "West Germany: The Economic Miracle". By way of comparison, it begins by stating that "no country in Europe since the war has so contrasted with Britain as the Federal Republic of Germany". Economic growth is described, and there is some brief analysis. Adenauer is mentioned, as is Erhard and Kiesinger. Adenauer is discussed for his hard-line stance toward the Soviet Union and eastern Europe. The Hallstein Doctrine is mentioned. Adenauer's refusal to recognize the German Democratic Republic may have "contributed to the Cold War climate" and „may have led the United States to overestimate the threat of communist aggression in Europe". The *Ostpolitik* of Willy Brandt is deseribed as "in part a subdivision of the policy of détente" between the United States and the Soviet Union. West Germany is also portrayed as pushing vigorously for better cooperation and greater unity between the west European members of NATO and the Common Market. There is discussion of government structure or of the differences between political parties although the SPD is described as having departed from socialism to become a party of social and economic reform. Schmidt is mentioned as the successor to Brandt.

Langer, William L.; Eadie, John W.; Geanakoplos, Deno J.; Hexter, J. H.; Pipes, Richard. *Western Civilization*. 2nd ed. New York: Harper and Row, 1975.

International Affairs: The authors of this book appear very interested in the spread of communism during the post-World War II period and the strength and nature of the Western response to that advance. The formation of the Federal Republic of Germany and the frequent problems over Berlin are discussed in detail. The Federal Republic is seen in terms of the apprehension that the reappearance of a strong German state creates for both the Soviet Union and France. The Soviets wish to prevent any future German aggression while the United States seeks a strong central European ally to contain communist aggression.

Government and Society: There are general sections in a chapter on European postwar developments. The various European states are comparatively analyzed in a most superficial fashion. The discussion of West German politics is very brief and concerned mostly with the differences between the East and West German states. Adenauer is mentioned as head of the Christian Democratic Party and chancellor of West Germany, but there is no discussion of his policies or personality. Brandt is not mentioned at all. The West German constitution is said to be "based upon that of Weimar". Finally, a description of the formation of East Germany is followed by an attempt to show the Federal Republic's greater popularity because of the many Germans who flee from East to West Germany each year. A substantial section on the Common Market discusses European economic growth. Individual countries are given only passing reference, and much is made of change in the attitude of European businessmen to a more "American" perspective – to try to develop consumer spending rather than seize a share of the existing market. In general, the post-World War II period seems to be an afterthought in this relatively new textbook.

McKay, John P.; Hill, Bennett D.; Buckler, John. *A History of Western Society*. Boston: Houghton Mifflin Company, 1979.

International Affairs: The aim of this discussion is to set the stage for the formation of the "new" Europe by describing the East-West ideological pressures to which the continent is subjected and to which it must adapt. The individual sketch of each nation is then fitted into this framework.

Government and Society: Politically, post-war Europe turned away from old leaders and ideologies discredited by the war and began to turn to revitalized and progressive Catholic parties – the Christian Democrats. In West Germany, this meant the rise of Konrad Adenauer. After political stability, European nations sought economic growth; West Germany, under the direction of Erhard as Minister of Economics, gambled by breaking from the heavily regulated Nazi economy to institute a free-market system. The tremendous success of this gamble brought renewed respect to free-market capitalism and stimulated trade and development within the entire west European economic system. This discussion then offers a device for describing the Common Market and its contribution to European prosperity and European unity.

Most of the remainder of the book describes the changing nature of west European society. Society is described as more mobile and more democratic as old class barriers break down. A new international class of civil servants and salaried managers in state-run enterprises has arisen across Europe to replace the old middle class of small independent businessmen. These people are highly trained technicians and specialists concerned with efficiency and economic growth. Their approach to most problems is realistic and pragmatic. West Germany shares this group and their outlooks with the other states of western Europe. West Germany does not share as fully the recent trend toward student unrest and left wing terrorism afflicting some other European states (see date of publication). – In general, this is a successful comparative approach, which treats the Federal Republic within the European spectrum and seeks to describe and analyze various political, social, economic, and cultural developments. The student has a better perception of Europe in the postwar period than most books in this category.

CATEGORY C

Chambers, Mortimer, Grew, etc. *The Western* Experience. 2nd ed. New York: Alfred A. Knopf, 1979.

The formation of the Federal Republic out of East-West disagreement and the continuing disruption of Berlin are woven into a general discussion of the "survival of Europe" after the World War and the Cold War.

Government and Society: The main theme here is West Germany's rise to world respectability through a stable democratic government and a strong capitalistic economy. The political and economic development of West Germany is used to explain the country's rise to a key position in modern Europe. Politically, West Germany prospered "in an atmosphere of efficient calm" under the conservative leadership of Adenauer. The new constitution strongly resembled Weimar, but the West German state was more compact, centralized, and politically stable than Weimar. This is one of the few textbooks to refer to a federal structure. Adenauer cultivated close relations with the United States and the ancient enemy France, but by doing so cost the nation something in chances for reunification with East Germany. Brandt moved to correct this situation through his *Ostpolitik* which not only opened relations with east Germany, but also eased tensions with the Soviet Union and Poland. Political questions, however, were always subordinated to the West German drive for prosperity. Even the Social Democrats, in power since 1969, have not lessened "the commitment to encouraging investment, expanding trade, and preventing inflation". "Only slightly less conservative" than their opponents, the Social Democrats' most venturesome economic measure requires worker representation on the boards of directors of the largest firms. All of this carefully nurtured political and economic strength has turned the outcast of Europe into one of the continent's leading and most envied powers. Brandt's *Ostpolitik* only became possible once both East and West Germany acquired some measure of economic clout and political respectability. A certain independence born of success gave Brandt his chance to take a diplomatic risk. These presentations are woven into two chapters, the second entitled "The Present in Historical Perspective", and West Germany generally appears together with France and Britain and/or Italy in discussing the revival of Europe. The Common Market receives extensive treatment and there are many tables and charts comparing television licenses, telephones, medical expenses paid through state plans, and other consumer and social indices across the world so that the reader can locate the relative position of West Germany in each case. There is a serious attempt to discuss social and economic circumstances across all of Europe within a comparative and analytical framework and to place the cultural elements and sources of discontent in perspective. This is a different approach from all of the other texts. A European perspective is sought, to examine the salient features of European society in the present era.

The general impression that one gains from an examination of these widely used texts is that the treatment of the Federal Republic of Germany is minimal at best. This is at least partly misleading. The western civilization textbooks compress two thousand years of history into one thousand pages. Few subjects receive extensive treatment, and most are presented in a brief form which serves to describe and add some features for analysis without appearing to be a catalogue of names, dates, and events. As a basic reference text for a general introductory course, little more can be done. In this sense, the Federal Republic receives no less attention than the Fourth and Fifth French Republics or the United Kingdom in the same context. In their effort to compress the history of the Federal Republic into a few paragraphs, or even a few pages, some authors have used a few descriptions which are inaccurate. Here and there, incorrect facts or statements appear. These can be corrected in revised editions. Far more serious, however, is the method of treatment of the entire post-World War II period. Even in the context of the purpose of these textbooks, this period receives too few pages of coverage. Newer textbooks are expanding this somewhat, but a good approach seems to be that of Chambers, which offers a comparative analysis that may be of real use to students. It is difficult, however, to escape the conclusion that the Federal Republic of Germany does in fact receive too little coverage in most American western civilization textbooks to permit college and university students to obtain an understanding of a country so important in world affairs today and so significantly a part of the future of the United States. In some fashion, the authors of currently used western civilization texts ought to rethink their approach to the Europe of today, and with it the Federal Republic of Germany, to present a valid picture, accurate and complete enough for the student to recognize contemporary society.

Gerald R. Kleinfeld

The Federal Republic of Germany in American College and University Textbooks in United States History

At all colleges and universities in the United States, there is a basic introductory course in United States history. High school students have already taken several courses in United States history, but most college and university freshmen or sophomores (first and second year students) also elect or are required to study this additional one year course. Most major textbook publishers offer at least one basic text, and many offer two or three. Selection is made by the individual professors. The textbooks are broad in scope and average 800 to 950 pages in length. They are intended to be used alongside required anthologies, paperback books treating particular subjects, and suggested library reading lists. Thus, they are not the only required or suggested reading matter for the course.

Texts in United States history treat both domestic and international affairs. Typically, the international component is briefer than the domestic. All texts reach to the present era, and most are revised frequently to bring them up to date. This compares most favorably with Western Civilization textbooks, which are not generally revised as often.

The treatment of the Federal Republic of Germany in United States history texts is quite limited. The origins and early years of the Federal Republic are depicted in those sections of the textbooks which consider(s) the final events of World War II and the international negotiations following that conflict. Thus, the Federal Republic emerges in the chapter(s) which consider the Cold War and U.S.-Soviet relations. The period of German history following the establishment of the Federal Republic is characteristically developed in sections of chapters which refer to NATO, to United States-European relations, to the Soviet Union and the Berlin crises, and to economic matters in terms of the Common Market. West German domestic events are rarely discussed, as might be expected. The key questions are those of U.S.-German relations or the role of Germany in the U.S.-Europe or U.S.-Soviet relations. Domestic German events are left to other books or to other courses. Nevertheless, because of the importance of United States-German relations over the last thirty years, it is useful to analyze the coverage of these events and of German affairs in general in basic United States history textbooks. This is especially true because far more students enroll in these courses than in the Western Civilization courses, where German history is presented in greater detail.

The following is a general analysis of the treatment of the Federal Republic of Germany in the most widely used textbooks for courses in United States history. The topics indicated are those in which the textbook authors have included reference to Germany since 1945.

(A) Bailey, Thomas A., and Kennedy, David M. *The American Pageant: A History of the Republic.* 2 vols. 6th ed. Lexington, Mass.: D. C. Heath & Co., 1979. 950 pg.

References to domestic German affairs

The authors mention the percentage of West German Gross National Product paid as taxes, which they depict in a graph showing several industrialized countries.

What is covered and how treated

Postwar De-militarization and de-industrialization: The purpose of de-militarization and de-industrialization was to prevent another German aggression. These policies were abandoned ". . . partly because Germany was the key to the economic recovery of Europe".

Nuremberg War Trials: The authors mention some of the crimes, the number of persons convicted, and Göring's suicide. They are supportive of the trials, although they report that there were some Americans who referred to them as "judicial lynching".

Allied estrangement over Germany: Soviet obstruction and refusal to work under a multi-power shell and Soviet attempts to impoverish Germany by means of reparations are presented. These Soviet policies had the purpose of making the Soviet Zone "prey to the seductive promises of Soviet Communism" and to forestall any future German aggression. Despite the Potsdam agreement to treat Germany as economic whole, the authors stress Soviet reluctance to lose control of East Germany and Austria by concluding multipower settlements.

Map showing partition zones: No descriptive/explanatory caption.

Soviet blockade of Berlin and Berlin Airlift: The authors discuss the Berlin question as a factor in the Cold War. They describe the partition of Berlin and the failure of the Western allies to provide for access to West Berlin. The authors praise allied resolution in organizing the Berlin Airlift, and claim a moral victory when the Soviets backed down. They state that these developments resulted in the formation of two Germanies, "Communist-dominated East Germany and the democratically organized West Germany".

Entrance into NATO and rearmament: This subject is mentioned in context of the support by the United States for France in Indo-China. The French were to be convinced by such support to accept German rearmament. The formation of the Warsaw Pact is cited as the Soviet reaction.

Berlin Wall: Khrushchev threatened to sign a treaty with East Germany and to cut western access to Berlin. Kennedy called up reserves and asked for an increase in the defense budget. Then the Soviets began construction of the Berlin Wall " to plug heavy population drain from East Germany to West Germany".

Point of view: All references of Germany are made in terms of increased tensions and growing estrangement between the United States and Europe as such.

(B) Bailyn, Bernard, et al. *The Great Republic: A History of the American People.* Lexington, Mass.: D. C. Heath & Co., 1977. 939 pg.

References to domestic German affairs

None.

What is covered and how treated

Yalta Conference: In the context of a general analysis of the Yalta Conference, Bailyn presents a description of the Soviet demands for heavy reparations and of Allied plans for a Germany stripped of the potential to make war.

Division into zones of occupation: The United States reconsidered earlier plans for harsh peace and decided that it would be best to treat the various occupation zones as self-contained units in order to shield the western part of Germany from Soviet demands.

Potsdam Conference: Briefly discussed.

Estrangement over German Issue: The Marshall Plan is described and its application to Germany is presented as important for the rebuilding of the German economy as well as a step towards the integration of Germany into a "free Europe". Truman's policy of reconciliation with Germany was viewed by the Soviets as an attack on their vital interests. A permanent division was thereby created between the Soviet and the western occupation zones.

Soviet blockade of Berlin and Berlin Airlift: The reasons for this Soviet action are not given. No mention is made of the status of Berlin. The Federal Republic of Germany is said to evolve from the western zones "and set on its way to independence". The German Democratic Republic is mentioned briefly as having been established.

Entrance into NATO and rearmament: The United States urged the western Europe states to rearm and merge their strength.

Berlin Crisis: Khrushchev threatened to restrict western access to Berlin. Bailyn explains that Khrushchev planned to use the Berlin issue to force a western recognition of East Germany. The Soviet leader also hoped to compel the West to agree to a new status for West Berlin.

Berlin Wall: The Soviets erected the wall in order to prevent dissidents from leaving East Germany. Kennedy called up military reserves, increased the United States garrison in Berlin, and proposed an increase in military spending. "By 1962 neither side wished to press the other on the issue of Berlin . . . [The] United States sought to preserve status quo."

Point of view: Most references to Germany are made in relation to United States-Soviet tension. There is considerable coverage of the development of wartime plans for postwar Germany. Bailyn mentions the formation of two German states and gives the proper names for them.

(C) Blum, John M., et al. *The National Experience: A History of the United States.* 4th ed. N. Y.: Harcourt, Brace, Jovanovich, 1977. 848 pg.

References to domestic German affairs

The authors mention Willy Brandt and describe him as being in the forefront of opposition to the spread of Stalinism in Europe while leading Germany towards ratification of treaties with Russia and Poland in 1972 (Ostpolitik).

What is covered and how treated

Postwar planning: The Morgenthau Plan is outlined and explained. German dismemberment was considered, but was abandoned. A European Advisory Commission instead proposed Allied zones of occupation. Blum points out the location of the occupation zones and the failure to settle the question of access to Berlin. The authors explain that divided Berlin lay within the Soviet zone. They discuss occupation policy in a limited fashion.

Map of partition zones: No descriptive caption.

Occupation of Germany: Each nation was to supervise its own zone but participate in an Allied Control Council. "Objectives of occupation were disarmament, a de-militarization, de-Nazification and encouragement of libertarian ideals." Troops were forbidden to fraternize and war crimes trials were instituted. However, the "occupation had begun in severity and, as circumstances changed, became progressively more benign".

Estrangement over German Issue: Through mutual suspicion any collaboration over postwar settlement on Germany became impossible. The respective sides began fostering a German rebirth in their own zones in order to fill the power vacuum. The German Federal Republic was established in the west and a German Democratic Republic in the east.

Soviet blockade of Berlin and the Berlin Airlift: The Soviet cut off all Western access to Berlin in an attempt to force the West out of Berlin. (No underlying causes are given.) An airlift was instituted, because the alternative of backing down would encourage the Soviets, while breaking the blockade by sending armed convoys through would trigger war. The blockade convinced Europeans of the need for regional defense.

NATO and German rearmament: The European allies were persuaded by the United States to permit a rearming of West Germany. Dulles' fear that a reduction in tension would cause the West to drop its guard caused him to reject significant Soviet proposals in 1953–54 after Stalin's death, most notably a neutralization of Germany.

Berlin Crisis: Khrushchev tried to keep nuclear weapons out of West Germany, reopening the Berlin question in October-November 1958. This resulted in a deadlock. To stop the flow of refugees to the West Khrushchev announced the Soviet intention to sign a peace treaty with East Germany, thus nullifying Soviet promises and enabling East Germany to cut the access to Berlin. In response, Kennedy called up army reserves. Khrushchev then postponed the treaty deadline in October and the crisis subsided. The construction of the Berlin Wall is mentioned.

Cuban missile crisis: Khrushchev cited missiles in Cuba to use as a bargaining chip to oust the West from Berlin.

Point of view: The German developments again revolve around United States-Soviet rivalry, but Berlin is the focal point. There is substantial coverage of planning for postwar Germany. The two Germanies are mentioned by name, and many details not mentioned in other books are cited (EEC, Oder-Neisse line, ACC, power vacuum, Soviet 1953–54 proposals, Cuban missile crisis).

(D) Graebner, N. A., et al. *A History of the American People*. 2nd ed. N. Y.: McGraw-Hill, 1975. 919 pg.

References to domestic German affairs

None.

What is covered and how treated

Disagreements over postwar planning: Discussion in this section centers on questions of occupation zones and the future of Berlin. Churchill argued that the boundaries of proposed occupation zones should not influence military operations and that possession of Berlin by the Soviets would make them more intractible. Graebner maintains that the failure of the allies to come to a general understanding with the USSR before returning to zones of occupation was very significant. Specifically, the question of western access to the "island" of Berlin was not settled. Stalin was permitted to insist that western access to Berlin was a privilege and not a right.

Potsdam Conference: "Stalin employed every possible device to maintain a maximum degree of Soviet prestige, power, and maneuverability." It was agreed that Germany should be de-militarized, de-Nazified and democratized. As reparations, the occupying powers were free to remove property for their own use and to seize German assets abroad.

Estrangement over Germany: The victors shared no fundamental purposes and could not agree on treatment of Germany. The USSR drained the eastern zone of factories and resources while the West rethought its policies. The Soviet Union organized the eastern zone as a satellite, and refused the proposal of Secretary of State Byrnes in September 1946 for reunification of Germany, maintaining that only Soviet terms were acceptable. The continuing quarrel over Germany led to a complete breakdown of the wartime alliance.

Nuremberg Trials: Graebner explains the nature of the charges, number of Nazis convicted and the purpose of the trials. The authors mention that there was some condemnation of the trial because of its *ex post facto* nature.

Soviet blockade of Berlin and Berlin Airlift: There is a sketchy treatment. The book mentions only that there was a Soviet blockade in response to the western decision to organize their three zones into a West German state, and that there was a successful airlift.

NATO and German rearmament: According to this text, "NATO transformed American occupation forces in Germany into defenders of Western Europe against a possible Soviet attack". In retaliation, the Soviets established an East German state and the Warsaw Pact. The decision to rearm West Germany had been blocked prior to 1954 by French fear of a revitalized German military power. Dulles' warning that continued French opposition "would compel an agonizing reappraisal of the basic United States policy" had convinced the French to give in.

Berlin Crisis: Khrushchev demanded that the West accept the neutralization of Berlin within six months. If the West refused, Russia would turn its zone over to East Germany, thus forcing the western allies to deal with a country whose existence they did not officially recognize. When the West stood firm, Khrushchev silently permitted the deadline to pass.

Berlin Wall: Khrushchev again demanded that the allies leave Berlin and threatened to turn control over to East Germany. Kennedy called up military reserves. The East Germans sealed off the border to stop the flood of refugees. "The future of West Berlin remained the key to the East-West struggle in Europe. For the Soviets the city was the pawn to compel formal Western acceptance of a divided Germany. For the United States West Berlin remained a symbol of Europe's will to hold the line against communism."

Point of view: The coverage of German affairs in Graebner centers around United States-Soviet antagonism and the tensions created by Berlin. Although the book mentions the two Germanies, it does not give their official names. There is a relatively substantial coverage of postwar agreements and negotiations.

(E) Garraty, J. A. *The American Nation*. 4th ed. N. Y.: Harper & Row, 1979. 804 pg.

References to domestic German affairs

None.

What is covered and how treated

Potsdam Conference: Garraty reports the agreement to hold war crimes trials, to make reparations plans, and to divide Germany into zones of occupation along with Berlin, "deep in the Soviet zone".

Soviet blockade of Berlin and Berlin Airlift: The West abandoned a "self-defeating" policy which would crush Germany for many years and instituted currency reforms while announcing plans to consolidate their zones into an autonomous West German state. The Soviets closed off access to Berlin and the Allies were faced with the prospect of either abandoning the city or fighting their way in. The United States instituted a Berlin airlift. This put the Soviets in the uncomfortable position of either starting a conflict or giving up the blockade. It was a victory for Truman's containment policy.

Map of partition zones: With descriptive caption.

Berlin Wall: Khrushchev closed the border in order to cut off the flow of refugees from East Germany. Because Kennedy did not order the United States to tear down the wall, Khrushchev became convinced that he could pursue aggressive tactics with impunity.

Point of view: No clear picture of United States policy towards Germany emerges because of a very uneven coverage of events relating to German affairs. The German participation in NATO receives only one sentence, but the reunification question is mentioned several times. The Berlin blockade is covered, but there is little on subsequent Berlin crises. The current state of U.S.-German relations does not appear.

(F) Unger, Irwin. *These United States: The Questions of Our Past.* Boston, Mass.: Little, Brown, and Co., 1978. 933 pg.

References to domestic German affairs

German postwar social conditions are mentioned, as well as the impact of the Marshall Plan, and German participation in detente through *Ostpolitik*.

What is covered and how treated

Postwar condition of Germany: Western Europe emerged from World War II no longer a great power center. It was shaken and enfeebled. German society was shattered. "Children begged on the streets and women sold themselves to American G.I.'s or Soviet soldiers for packs of cigarettes and chocolate bars."

Photograph page 859: Shows Nurembergers sitting in makeshift shelters in the ruins of their city.

Marshall Plan: This was created to stiffen European resistance to Soviet and internal Communist pressures. The West was determined to restore an independent German state, to stabilize German currency, and to create a West German Federal Republic. The Federal Republic ultimately created a German Marshall Fund to support cultural exchange between the United States and Europe.

Soviet blockade of Berlin and Berlin Airlift: In fear of a strong and militant Germany, the Soviets imposed a blockade of Berlin. The United States instituted an airlift of vital supplies until the Soviets finally backed down. Berlin remained a Western hostage in Soviet-East German hands, periodically triggering dangerous crises, until 1971.

NATO: A list of NATO members does not include the Federal Republic of Germany, and there is no later reference to German membership in NATO.

Paris Summit, 1959: Eisenhower's refusal to discuss the U-2 incident caused Khrushchev to break off the Paris summit meeting where Berlin and divided Germany were to be discussed.

Khrushchev-Kennedy Vienna Summit and Berlin Crises: The two leaders met to iron out differences over Berlin. Khrushchev demanded that the West withdraw from Berlin, otherwise Russia would sign a separate peace with East Germany and place its military might behind the East German claim to the city. Kennedy refused to be intimidated, called up military reserves and asked for an increase in the defense budget. The Soviets then threatened to mobilize. East German authorities replied by building the Berlin Wall, to prevent further refugee flights to the west. The crisis abated when Khrushchev postpone indefinitely a peace treaty with the German Democratic Republic. The problem of Berlin and the two Germanies was settled by the Berlin accord of 1971. Britain, France, the United States, the Union of Soviet Socialist Republics, and West and East Germany agreed to improve communications between Berlin and West Germany.

Point of view: Described from the viewpoint of Russian-American antagonism, this book provides uneven coverage. Not mentioned are the Potsdam Conference, the Nuremberg War Crimes Trials, German entry into NATO, and German rearmament. However, Unger does discuss the loss of German territory to Poland. He mentions immediate postwar social conditions in Germany and the 1959 aborted Paris Summit Conference. This is the only text to mention the German Marshall Fund. The discussion on Berlin Crisis is very brief. On page 916, the author writes that in "1971 the perennial problem of Berlin and the two Germanies was finally settled by the Berlin Accord . . . [in which the former wartime allies] legitimize the existence of two distinct German nations".

(G) Weinstein, Allen, and Wilson, R. Jackson. *Freedom and Crisis: An American History.* 2nd ed. N. Y.: Random House, 1978. 948 pg.

Although the Federal Republic of Germany is included in a list of members of the Common Market and in other such isolated references, this textbook does not discuss any aspect of the history of the Federal Republic of Germany in the presentation of postwar United States foreign relations. There is no discussion of NATO or the Berlin Crises, or of United States-European relations.

There are individual deficiencis in each of the textbooks considered, of course, but one cannot fault the authors for failing to treat the history of the Federal Republic of Germany extensively in textbooks designed for United States history courses. The books are designed for another purpose – to present the history of the United States and its relationship to the other states of the world community. It is in considering this purpose that one should analyze and determine what has been done. Irrespective of individual faults and positive factors, all of the books cited exhibit two main problems with respect to Germany which cry out for resolution in terms of the stated purpose of the books themselves.

The first problem is that no picture of the Federal Republic of Germany, or of any other European state, or of Europe itself emerges from these books. The student sees German events in the context of superpower rivalry but has no opportunity to know or to understand the nature of the German society itself. This is crucial for the second problem, which is the total absence of any consideration of United States-German relations and United States-Europe relations. It is clearly within the framework of these books to consider the present and future state of United States economic and political development in the international sphere. This glaring ommission leaves it to other courses and other books to inform the student of United States history of the nature of an interdependency that has arisen since World War II and the nature of the states and societies in western Europe with this interdependency has been established.

